CALVIN

ABINGDON PILLARS
OF THEOLOGY

230
Stroup

CALVIN

George Stroup

Abingdon Press
Nashville

CALVIN

This book is printed on acid-free paper.

Library of Congress Cataloging-in-Publication Data

Stroup, George W., 1944-
 Calvin / George Stroup.
  p. cm. (Abingdon pillars of theology ; v. 7)
 Includes bibliographical references and index.
 ISBN 978-0-687-65913-5 (pbk. : alk. paper)
  1. Calvin, Jean, 1509-1564. 2. Calvinism. 3. Reformed Church—Doctrines—History—16th century.
 I. Title.

 BX9418.S93 2009
 230'.42—dc22
 [B]
                                        2009011231

All scripture quotations unless noted otherwise are taken from the *New Revised Standard Version of the Bible*, copyright 1989, Division of Christian Education of the National Council of the Churches of Christ in the United States of America. Used by permission. All rights reserved.

The Hebraica® and Graeca® fonts used to print this work are available from Linguist's Software, Inc., PO Box 580, Edmonds, WA 98020-0580 tel (206) 775-1130.

09 10 11 12 13 14 15 16 17 18—10 9 8 7 6 5 4 3 2 1

MANUFACTURED IN THE UNITED STATES OF AMERICA

CONTENTS

PREFACE

July 10, 2009, is the five hundredth anniversary of John Calvin's birth. For half a millennium he has been a major figure in Christian theology, not only because of the pivotal role he played in the Protestant Reformation of the sixteenth century, but also because he has continued to influence theology, the church, and Western society. Longevity, however, does not necessarily breed familiarity. Down through the years historians and biographers have discovered many different Calvins. To some he was a prolific theologian, a commentator on the Bible, and a preacher, to whom other theologians, European royalty, politicians, and church leaders wrote for guidance about Christian faith and advice on how to form a Christian society. To others he was an austere, joyless, narrow-minded autocrat who ruled Geneva with an iron fist. He was many things to many people, but regardless of how one assesses him it would be difficult to deny his influence in the sixteenth century and his continuing significance today.

In this brief essay about Calvin I have attempted to do three things. First, I have tried to place him in his historical context. Too often he is read as a "disembodied" theologian—that is, without regard to his context—who wrote a large book about theology and many biblical commentaries and sermons, but about whom the reader knows very little. As with most theologians, what Calvin wrote cannot be reduced to his biography and his personal experiences, but it is equally a mistake to attempt to read him apart from the life he lived and his historical context. The theology Calvin wrote in Geneva is inseparable from the live he lived there.

Second, because this Pillars of Theology series is a brief introduction to major theologians for people reading them for the first time, I have tried to allow Calvin to speak in his own voice. There is now a consensus in Calvin scholarship that his lectures and commentaries on the Bible and his sermons, letters, and occasional essays are just as important for understanding him as is his major work, *Institutes of the Christian Religion*. Calvin tells his readers that because the *Institutes* is "the sum of religion in all its parts" it is not necessary for him to undertake lengthy doctrinal discussions in his commentaries on Scripture. The *Institutes* is a guide to the content of Scripture, but it also cannot be fully understood apart from Calvin's biblical commentaries and sermons. Given the limited scope of this essay and because I want those reading Calvin for the first time to have some sense of the coherence of his theology, I have focused primarily on the *Institutes*.

Third, Calvin is a "pillar" because theologians have continued to appeal to him as they wrestled with the issues of their day. Some Calvin scholars have pointed out the danger of reading Calvin through the eyes of those who have used him for their own purposes. That danger is indeed real. We must struggle to hear Calvin himself and not focus on what others have said about him or the uses they have made of him. Equally unfortunate, however, are attempts to build a "firewall" between Calvin and issues in contemporary life and theology. He is a pillar because he continues to have significance for social, political, and theological issues that did not exist in his day, but that significance requires interpretation and interpretation is never mere repetition.

Finally, Calvin was a sixteenth-century man who reflected his times, culture, and society. A significant theme in his theology is the "fatherhood" of God, by which Calvin meant God's gracious love and continuing care for creation. No doubt some readers may prefer that the masculine imagery in his description of God be made gender inclusive. However, because I want the reader to hear Calvin in his own voice and not in the voice some of us may think he should have used, I have chosen not to alter what he wrote. At the same time, it is important to remember Calvin's warning that we not confuse human images with the holy reality of God.

Only a few theologians have had enduring significance. Their voices were not silenced by their graves. They continue to be read and discussed, not because they are timeless portraits in a theological hall of fame, but because they continue to illumine and challenge the experiences of others, and because they have been edifying for those who have followed them and who must deal with challenges they could not have imagined. I have tried to identify a few of the ways in which Calvin remains a living voice for those who continue to struggle with what Christian faith means for human life at the beginning of the twenty-first century.

Gratitude is both a Christian and a Calvinist virtue. I am grateful to the students who have sat in my classes the last thirty-five years and listened patiently as I tried to convince them it would be good for their souls to read Calvin. Calvin makes the case for himself far better than I have ever been able to. And I am deeply grateful to Professor Brian Gerrish of Union Theological Seminary in Richmond, Virginia, who was kind enough to read an early draft of this manuscript and saved me from errors too numerous to mention. But no doubt not all.

CHAPTER ONE

LIFE

Historians have been frustrated in their attempts to write Calvin's biography by his reticence. He tells us little about himself. Unlike Augustine, he left no *Confessions*; unlike Luther, no one recorded his *Table Talk*. Beginning in his early twenties, Calvin wrote prolifically (his collected works in the *Corpus Reformatorum* comprise fifty-nine volumes).[1] Between the publication of his first book in 1532 (when he was twenty-two) and his death in 1564, he wrote theological texts, commentaries on the Bible, sermons, catechisms, plans for church reorganization, and a large number of letters. But with the exception of some of his letters and a few comments elsewhere, he provides few insights into his personal feelings. We do not know his thoughts and feelings about his mother's death when he was very young, his father's request that he give up his studies in theology and turn to law, the excommunication of his father and older brother by the Catholic Church, or any romantic interests he may have had prior to his marriage in 1540 (when he was thirty-one). In his letters he does discuss the death of his wife, Idelette, to whom he was married for nine years, but we know few details about their relationship (except his gratitude she did not hinder his work), his thoughts and feelings on the death of his infant son, or the adultery of his sister-in-law, who lived in his home. His letters provide some insight into his feelings about his expulsion from Geneva in 1538, his struggle over whether to return there in 1541, and his victory over his political opponents in 1555, but not enough for a biographer to reconstruct the emotional life of the man behind the events. Only in a few texts does Calvin write autobiographically and even then somewhat elusively, as though he considered it inappropriate to focus on himself rather than God.

The one text in which Calvin does write about his life is the preface to his *Commentary on the Psalms*, written in 1557 when he was forty-eight and had only seven years left to live. Not surprisingly historians have pored over this text, but with only limited results. Of particular interest is his reference to an event that happened much earlier in his life, a "sudden" or "unexpected" conversion in which God turned his hardened mind to docility and gave him a taste of what he refers to as "true piety." Unlike Augustine, he does not tell us when or where this event occurred or under what circumstances, whether it was a single, dramatic event or a gradual change in his understanding of his vocational calling.

Furthermore, the first biographies of Calvin were written by people who either revered or despised him. Soon after his death in 1564 the debate over Calvin began between those who understood him to be one of the giants in the history of Christian theology, who transformed the city of Geneva into what the Scottish theologian John Knox described as "the most perfect school of Christ that ever was in the earth since the days of the Apostles,"[2] and those who viewed him as a narrow-minded bigot, legalistic and autocratic, a tyrant, who from 1536 until 1564 subjected the people of Geneva to a reign of religious terror, tolerated no dissent, and because of his role in the execution of Michael Servetus in 1553, had blood on his hands.[3] Theodore Beza, his colleague for sixteen years in Geneva and his first biographer, wrote that "in him all men may see a most beautiful example of the Christian character, an example which it is as easy to slander as it is difficult to imitate," while a recent, late–twentieth-century biographer describes him as "an unhappy man, with whom it is difficult for the modern reader to feel any great bond of sympathy."[4]

In order to better understand both Calvin and the tradition that bears his name, we cannot help searching for the "historical Calvin," even if he is maddeningly uncooperative in the quest. Although his biographers disagree about the precise dating of events, Calvin's life invites division into four periods: first, from 1509 to 1536, his birth, education, and emergence as a leader of church reform; second, from 1536 to 1538, his first attempt, with Guillaume Farel and Pierre Viret, to reform the church and civic life of Geneva and their expulsion; third, from 1538 to 1541, his move to Strasbourg at Martin Bucer's invitation to serve as the minister to a French refugee congregation; and fourth, from 1541 to 1564, his return to Geneva to reform its church and civic life until his death on May 27, 1564, at the age of 54.

Childhood, Education, and Conversion (1509–1536)

Born Jean Cauvin on July 10, 1509, in Noyon, in the region of Picardy in northern France, fifty-eight miles northeast of Paris, he was twenty-five years younger than Martin Luther (1483–1546) and Huldrych Zwingli (1484–1531), eighteen years younger than Martin Bucer (1491–1551), and along with Heinrich Bullinger (1504–1575) and Philip Melanchthon (1497–1560), a member of the "second generation" of Protestant Reformers. He was only eight years old in 1517 when Luther wrote his 95 Theses in Wittenberg.

Much of what we know about Calvin's early life comes from the first biographies written about him, and their historical accuracy is uncertain. His father, Gerard Cauvin, was born in 1454 and settled in Noyon in 1481, eventually found employment with the bishop, Charles de Hangest, and became an administrative official for the cathedral chapter of Noyon. Toward the end of his life, Gerard ran afoul of the church over financial disputes and died excommunicated in 1531. Little is known about Calvin's mother, Jeanne Le Franc, except that she died in about 1515 when Calvin was five or six and was known for her piety. Calvin had an older brother, Charles, who received holy orders but was excommunicated and died in 1537, two other brothers, Antoine and François, and two sisters, Marie and one whose name is unknown. What did Calvin look like? Beza describes him as "of moderate stature, of a pale and dark complexion, with eyes that sparkled to the moment of his death, and bespoke his great intellect."[5]

Calvin probably began to learn Latin as a youth at the College des Capettes in Noyon. In 1521, his father obtained his first benefice or scholarship from the cathedral, which helped finance his education for the next thirteen years until he resigned them in 1534. About 1523, when he was perhaps fourteen, Calvin moved to Paris to prepare for university studies and eventually the priesthood. He may have studied for a few months at the College de La Marche with the Latin scholar Maturin Cordier (who some thirty years later Calvin would bring to teach at the academy he established in Geneva).[6] He then moved to the College de Montaigu, which was founded in the early fourteenth century and where both Erasmus and Rabelais had been students. The school had a reputation for its strict academic life and severe living conditions. He studied what today we would describe as "liberal arts" courses, such as grammar, rhetoric, and logic.

In 1527 his father became embroiled in a dispute with the leaders of the cathedral chapter in Noyon and advised his son to change his vocational plans from the priesthood to law. That same year Calvin moved first to Orleans, where he studied with Pierre de l'Estoile, and then in 1529 to Bourges in order to study with the Italian jurist Andrea Alciati and the Greek scholar Melchior Wolmar. Calvin's legal education was not like that of modern law students. Jurisprudence was not the study of case law but a branch of humanist studies, with the emphasis on grammar, philology, and logic. In his formal education, between 1523 and 1531, Calvin learned the tools and methods of humanism, equipment that would later serve him well in Strasbourg and Geneva as a lecturer on Scripture and as a preacher and theologian.

"Humanism" here does not mean a worldview that emphasizes the human and rejects the existence of God. Late Renaissance humanism is not the "godless atheism" so frequently denounced in contemporary American politics, but a style of thinking that values classical languages such as Latin, Greek, and Hebrew and the study of Greek philosophers such as Plato and Aristotle and Roman figures such as Cicero and Seneca. Humanists believed that many important problems were best understood if one could recover the wisdom of the ancients. Perhaps the best known humanists in Calvin's day were Jacques Lefèvre d'Etaples (1455–1536) and Desiderius Erasmus (1469–1536). In the 1520s the latter published two editions of a commentary on the Roman Stoic philosopher Seneca's treatise on clemency, *De Clementia*. In April 1532, Calvin published his own commentary on that text in an attempt to add material he believed Erasmus had neglected and in so doing establish himself as a rising star in the world of humanist scholarship. Apparently Calvin even paid for the book's publication, which turned out to be an unwise investment. The book was not a success. Although historians have combed it for clues to Calvin's theology, there is no indication in it that he had joined those committed to the reform of the Catholic Church. What is evident is that in 1532, at the age of twenty-two, Calvin was deeply influenced by the humanism of his day. William Bouwsma argues that for the rest of his life, "Calvin inhabited the Erasmian world of thought and breathed its spiritual atmosphere; he remained in major ways always a humanist of the late Renaissance."[7]

In 1533 Calvin returned to Paris; and on November 1, All Saints Day, his friend Nicolas Cop, the new rector of the university, delivered the convocation address for the beginning of the academic year. Cop took as his text the Sermon on the Mount in Matthew 5 and argued that Christians are saved by faith and not by their works or merit, a theme identified with Luther and the emerging, controversial movement for church reform. In the furor that followed, both Cop and Calvin fled the city. Although Cop delivered the speech, a copy of it was found in Calvin's handwriting. Did he simply make a copy of the address for Cop or for himself, or did Calvin write part or all of the address? One reason biographers have been so interested in that question is that it is difficult to know precisely when Calvin left the Catholic Church and joined the movement for church reform. Once again, because of Calvin's reticence it is a difficult, perhaps impossible, question to answer.

In 1557, in his preface to his *Commentary on the Psalms*, Calvin described how some thirty years earlier, he began to experience true piety:

> by a sudden conversion [God] subdued and made teachable a heart which, for my age, was far too hardened in such matters. Having thus received some foretaste and knowledge of true piety, I was straightway inflamed with such great desire to profit by it, that although I did not attempt to give up other studies I worked only slackly at them.[8]

Understandably historians want to know what this "sudden conversion" was and when precisely it occurred. Was it a sudden event or simply an unexpected one? Was it a dramatic moment, like that of the Apostle Paul on the road to Damascus or Augustine sitting in a garden reading Romans 13:13-14, or a more gradual process of change? Was it a conversion of the mind from one way of understanding Christian faith to another, or was it not so much a change of thinking as a clarification of calling and vocation? Over the years Calvin scholars have offered various theories in response to these questions.[9] One thing seems clear. There is a significant change between the young, humanist scholar who wrote the commentary on Seneca in 1532 and the theologian who four years later published the first edition of his *Institutes*. Although Bouwsma may well be correct that Calvin never left his humanism behind, still the humanist scholar of 1532 had by 1536 become a promising young theologian whose interpretation of Christian faith clearly advocated the reform of the Catholic Church.

In May 1534, Calvin returned to Noyon for the final time. His father had died in 1531, and Calvin returned to resign his benefices from the cathedral. Some of his biographers see this decision as an indication that he had decided to join the movement for reform and that his "conversion" must, therefore, have been prior to May 1534.[10] On October 17 posters or "placards" written by Antoine Marcourt, pastor of Neuchâtel, appeared in several French cities, including the king's bedroom, protesting the Mass and the Catholic celebration of the Eucharist. A severe persecution of "the Lutheran sect" (as Francis I described it) followed, and in January 1535, Calvin fled to Basel where he wrote a preface to his cousin Pierre Robert Olivetan's French translation of the Bible, arguing that the Bible should be read and studied by all people, not just the learned. During this same period he was hard at work on the first edition of what he referred to as his "Latin catechism," the *Institution of the Christian Religion*, which is dated August 23, 1535, in the Preface but was not published in Basel until seven months later in March 1536.

In the same month the book was published Calvin traveled to Ferrara in Italy and then to Paris, where he settled his affairs and persuaded his brother and sister to follow him abroad. He intended to travel to Strasbourg and there resume his writing and scholarship, but because hostilities had broken out between Francis I and Charles V he was forced to take an extended detour south and east that led him to an evening's stay in Geneva. With the exception of three years in Strasbourg, what began as an evening's stay in Geneva turned into the rest of his life.

First Stay in Geneva (1536–1538)

In the same preface to his *Commentary on the Psalms* in which he describes his "conversion," Calvin also tells the story of what happened that evening in Geneva. Guillaume Farel, who had been in Geneva for almost four years, heard that Calvin was there and went to visit, urging him to remain and help reform the church and the city. Calvin tried to beg off, pleading that he wanted only to return to his scholarly work in Basel, but Farel insisted, telling him that God would curse him if he refused to stay and assist the cause. Remarkably, Calvin, who was not easily intimidated, reluctantly agreed.

Geneva was a city of approximately ten thousand people, which had only recently (in 1526), with the assistance of Bern, freed itself from the duchy of Savoy and its Catholic bishop, Pierre de la Baume. On May 25, 1536, the people of Geneva declared themselves to be a city of the movement for reform. It was an independent city governed by four "syndics" or magistrates, who were elected by the male citizens of the town, and a series of councils: a Petit or Little Council of twenty-five members, which met three times a week; a Council of Sixty; the Council of Two Hundred, which met monthly and elected the Petit Council; and the General Council, consisting of all male citizens, which met twice a year. This cumbersome political structure is significant because it indicates how inappropriate it is to describe Geneva during Calvin's years there as a theocracy. He was never a member of Geneva's governing councils or political parties. Most Genevans treasured their recently won political independence from Savoy and their ecclesial independence from Rome. Who would determine the structure of the church and how would the church and the city's councils sort out their respective spheres of authority in the lives of its citizens? As Calvin soon discovered these were not questions that would be answered easily or quickly or without great controversy.

Calvin was initially appointed a "reader" or lecturer on the Bible, but soon began to preach, engage in other pastoral tasks, and participate in the reorganization of the church. On November 10, 1536, Calvin and Farel submitted to the Little Council a *Confession of Faith which all the citizens and inhabitants of Geneva and the subjects of the country must promise to keep and hold.*[11] It identified the church of Jesus Christ as those assemblies in which "his holy gospel be purely and faithfully preached, proclaimed, heard, and kept" and "his sacraments be properly administered." Furthermore, it declared that because there are always some "who hold God and his Word in contempt . . . we hold the discipline of excommunication to be a thing holy and salutary among the faithful, since truly it was instituted by our Lord with good reason."[12] Excommunication served two purposes: it protected the church from being corrupted by unrepentant sinners, and it admonished and brought to repentance those who were unrepentant.

Two months later, on January 16, 1537, Farel and Calvin presented to the Little Council their *Articles Concerning the Organization of the Church and of Worship at*

Geneva,[13] which reorganized the church around four issues. The first concerned the Lord's Supper, which the *Articles* urged should be celebrated every Sunday "at least as a rule"; certainly not merely two or three times a year as had been recent practice in Geneva. Because the Supper should not be "soiled and contaminated by those coming to it," the church should establish "the correction and discipline of excommunication," as commanded by Jesus in Matthew 18,[14] by electing "certain persons of good life and witness" who would urge amendment on any person in whom they saw "any vice worthy of note" and, if rebuffed, report the offender to the ministers.[15]

Second, the *Articles* urged all the inhabitants of the city, beginning with the members of the Little Council, to "make confession of and give reason for their faith" by affirming *The Confession of Faith* submitted the previous year. In addition, psalms should be sung in worship because they "can incite us to lift up our hearts to God and move us to an ardour in invoking and exalting with praises the glory of his Name."[16]

Third, children should be instructed in Christian faith. This was particularly urgent because of "the contempt of parents in instructing their children in the way of God."[17] To that end Calvin wrote an *Instruction in Faith* consisting of thirty-three articles that begins with the assertion "All men are born in order to know God."[18] Finally, the *Articles* urge the creation of a commission that would deal with confusion and inconsistencies in laws governing marriage.

From the beginning the question of the relation between the governing councils and the church and its ministers was contentious. It is important to understand this argument from both sides. From the Genevans' perspective they had only recently freed themselves from the clutches of the Duke of Savoy and the Church of Rome and now Calvin and Farel wanted the people of Geneva to submit to the discipline of the Word of God in the Bible. No doubt this felt to many like simply exchanging one overbearing master for another. On the other side, Calvin and Farel understood the Bible to claim that all things should be made captive to Jesus Christ. As in many power struggles the issue was territory or political turf. What belonged to the domain of the civil government and what to the church and its ministers? Which matters were "political" and the business of the councils and which were "religious" and the province of the church and its ministers? Remember these were people who knew nothing of "the separation of church and state." In February 1538, supporters of Bern, antagonistic to Calvin and Farel, were elected to Geneva's councils. They favored the Bernese pattern of quarterly celebration of the Lord's Supper and rejected the ministers' request that it be celebrated at least monthly. The conflict soon escalated. The ministers preached on Easter Sunday but refused to celebrate the Eucharist. The following Tuesday they were ordered to leave Geneva within three days. Two years of work seemed to have been wasted.

Strasbourg (1538–1541)

After traveling from Geneva to Bern and then to Zürich, Calvin settled in Basel hoping to return finally to the quiet of his study. Those hopes were short-lived. Using tactics not unlike Farel's during Calvin's stop in Geneva in 1536, Martin Bucer persuaded Calvin to move to Strasbourg, where in September 1538 he become the pastor of a congregation of four to five hundred French refugees. The next three years appear to have been the happiest in Calvin's life. In Strasbourg he did not face the political problems that plagued him in Geneva. Bucer had been there for sixteen years (since 1522) and prior to Calvin's arrival had written ordinances for the church in Strasbourg, a catechism, and published a commentary on Romans in 1536, all of which strongly influenced Calvin's later work.

In addition to his daily duties as a pastor, including regular preaching, Calvin gave lectures on the Gospel of John and Paul's Letters to the Corinthians and in March 1540 published his first biblical commentary, on Paul's *Letter to the Romans*. In 1539 he published a revised and expanded edition of his *Institutes* (the 1539 edition consisting of seventeen chapters compared to six in the original 1536 edition) and in 1541 a French translation of the *Institutes*.

Also in 1539 Calvin accepted an invitation from the Council in Geneva to respond to a letter it had received from Cardinal Jacopo Sadoleto, bishop of Carpentras, urging the city to return to the Catholic Church. Like many debates in the sixteenth century, the debate between Calvin and Sadoleto was about authority. What is the final authority or norm for Christian faith and life? Sadoleto invoked the authority of the Pope and church tradition. All claims to authority, Calvin argued, must be tested by the Word of God; "in a word, let our church be one whose supreme concern it is humbly and religiously to venerate the Word of God, and submit in obedience to it."[19]

Calvin's life in Strasbourg was calmer, less tempestuous, than it had been in Geneva. He was busy with his duties as a pastor, preaching several times a week, teaching, and writing, but he still found time to participate with Bucer in several colloquies or conferences, organized by Emperor Charles V in an attempt to reconcile Catholics and the various reform movements. At these he met many of the leading theologians of his day, including Philip Melanchthon, whose *Loci Communes* (1521) he greatly admired.

In August 1540, Calvin, then thirty-one, married Idelette de Bure, the widow of a former Anabaptist and the mother of two children. The marriage lasted nine years, until Idelette's death in 1549. They had one son who died in infancy.

While Calvin was enjoying the tranquility of Strasbourg, controversy continued to plague Geneva. The church and the councils were divided between those who continued to support Calvin and his colleagues and those who supported the ministers who had replaced them. By September 1540 Calvin's opponents had lost their places on the council and two of the ministers who had replaced Calvin and Farel had left Geneva. In the vacuum the council began attempts to convince Calvin to return. Calvin wrote Farel he would rather die a hundred times than return to "the cross of Geneva," but, like Jonah, he was unable to escape the gnawing conviction that not just the councils of Geneva but God was calling him back to the city. In September 1541, Calvin, then thirty-two, returned to Geneva for the last time. The twenty-three years remaining in his life were given to the reconstruction of the church and the city according to what Calvin understood to be the Word of God. No doubt many wondered what Calvin would say his first Sunday back in the pulpit of Saint Pierre. He said nothing about the events of his departure or the intervening three years but simply resumed preaching from the text in Matthew's Gospel where he had concluded his final sermon in 1538.

Second Stay in Geneva (1541–1564)

As soon as he returned to Geneva Calvin began writing his *Ecclesiastical Ordinances of the Church of Geneva*, which he completed within a week and submitted to the councils. Once again the city's political leaders worried that Calvin's proposals expanded the power of the ministers and intruded on the prerogatives of the civil government. While Calvin agreed that the council had the right to confirm ministers selected by the consistory, the council insisted that it should also have a role in their selection. The *Ordinances* called for the pastors of the city to meet weekly to study the Bible and quarterly as "the company of pastors" to engage in self-criticism and mutual correction. Furthermore, the ministers together with twelve (and later eighteen) laymen or "elders" elected from the councils made up the consistory, which was responsible among other things for discipline in the church. The consistory was to engage in conversation with those whose lives were not in accordance with the gospel (for example, anyone who refused to attend worship), if necessary to admonish them, and if they refused to change their ways to refuse them admittance to the Lord's Supper and in the most recalcitrant of cases to excommunicate them from the life of the church until they repented.

The influence of Bucer during Calvin's time in Strasbourg is evident in the four offices of ministry established by the *Ordinances*: (1) pastors, whose calling was to preach the gospel, administer the sacraments, and participate in the disciplining of the congregation; (2) elders, who were charged with overseeing the life of the congregation and disciplining those who strayed from the gospel; (3) teachers, whose task was to instruct believers in correct doctrine derived from the Bible; and (4) deacons, who had responsibility for the church's administration and care of the poor and destitute. In each case these four "offices" of ministry were callings to specific tasks or functions within the life of the church. On November 20, 1541, two months after Calvin first submitted them, the *Ordinances* were approved by the councils.

Once again opposition to Calvin grew steadily in Geneva. In 1546 Pierre Ameaux claimed Calvin was preaching false doctrine. He was punished by the council and was forced to walk through the city bareheaded, carrying a torch and requesting forgiveness. Several prominent people in the city led the movement against Calvin, including Ami Perrin, who had been instrumental in arranging Calvin's return to Geneva from Strasbourg. One can imagine the resentment of these powerful people to the intrusion of Calvin and the rest of the consistory into what they probably considered their personal and private lives. In the election of 1548 those aligned with Perrin defeated the supporters of Calvin and the consistory. The political ground, however, was rapidly eroding beneath the Perrinists as growing numbers of refugees from France and Italy flooded into Geneva, straining both the city's resources and its hospitality. Some Genevans worried that the French refugees were taking over the city. In the elections of February 1555, after a significant number of French refugees had received citizenship, the Perrinists were defeated. The four magistrates now sided with Calvin, and the Perrinists lost their positions in the council. On May 16, Perrin and his supporters attempted to burn a house filled with French refugees, and in the riot that followed he and other leaders of the opposition fled the city. All significant opposition to Calvin evaporated. For the next nine years, until his death, Calvin faced few political obstacles to his attempts to reform the city. On Christmas, 1559, twenty-three years after arriving in the city, he was finally offered a form of Genevan citizenship.

While in Geneva Calvin was also involved in numerous theological controversies. Easily the best known of Calvin's theological opponents was the Spanish physician Michael Servetus, who made important contributions on the circulation of blood and in 1531 published two books on what he argued were errors in the doctrine of the Trinity. Because of his theological views Servetus worked under an assumed name as the physician to the archbishop at Vienne, but in 1545 he wrote Calvin a series of theological questions to which Calvin responded by sending him a copy of the *Institutes*. Servetus returned it with derogatory comments written in the margins—not a strategy designed to foster dialogue and mutual respect. Servetus's identity as the author of the books challenging the Trinity was eventually exposed, and he was arrested in Vienne, interrogated, and sentenced to be burned, but managed to escape from jail and flee the city. Inexplicably he decided to visit Geneva and while attending a worship service was recognized and arrested. He was tried by the Little Council, who consulted several Swiss cities for advice. The Perrinists attempted to use Servetus to score political points against Calvin but received no support from the other Swiss cities, and on October 26, 1553, Servetus was condemned to death. Calvin and the ministers urged a humane form of execution, such as beheading, but the following day he and his book were burned at the stake.

Servetus was by no means the only heretic to be executed in the sixteenth century. Sadly, blood was shed in the name of Jesus Christ by many Christian groups. And it was not just those who believed "wrongly" who were persecuted. In Geneva and throughout Europe plague and famine were events that evoked fear and scapegoating. In May 1545, seven men and twenty-four women in Geneva were accused of sorcery and spreading plague and were executed.[20] The Servetus affair left a lasting stain on Calvin's reputation, confirming for many the image of Calvin as the cold, severe, heartless tyrant of Geneva. Contemporary readers, shaped by Enlightenment values of tolerance and pluralism, often have difficulty understanding his role in Servetus's death. Calvin shared a conviction with many other theologians in the sixteenth century (both Catholic and Protestant) that heresy was not just a matter of poor judgment or wrong belief that threatened the soul of the heretic, but was a threat to the faith and life of the entire church, and as such even more dangerous than plague or famine. Hopefully few Christian theologians today would argue that heresy (or any other crime) deserves capital punishment. On the other hand, theologians like Calvin, Luther, and Zwingli (who participated in the drowning in Zurich of several Anabaptists) might have difficulty understanding the position, held by many Christians today, that faith is a purely private matter and has no implications for the life of the church or the larger community.

Calvin and the other ministers in Geneva were concerned not only with the reform of the church but with the life of the city as well. In 1546 the ministers attempted to have the city's taverns closed and replaced by houses equipped with a Bible, where prayers would be said before and after meals, cursing and dancing forbidden, and performances in the city's theaters censored. Apparently this experiment was no more well received then than it would be today, and lasted only a few months. While this attempt to control behavior may sound quaint, even strange, today to those who live in secular, pluralistic Western democracies in which religion in almost any form is voluntary and personal, it is important to remember that these "reforms" were not imposed on an unwilling public by a zealous clergy, but were implemented by both the consistory and the governing councils.

Perhaps the most important social reform during Calvin's time in Geneva was the establishment of the academy in 1559, only five years before Calvin's death. A school in some form had existed in Geneva since the fourteenth century, but during the early days of the city's commitment to reform the school had not fared well. Finally, in 1558 the council committed the city to the construction of an academy, which was officially dedicated in June 1559 and was finally completed in 1563. Calvin was able to assemble an impressive faculty, including Theodore Beza as rector, and several established scholars in Greek, Latin, and Hebrew, including Calvin's former teacher, Mathurin Cordier. At the time of Calvin's death there were about one thousand students taking the basic course of study at the academy and about three hundred preparing for the ministry, medicine, or law. Many who became ministers were then sent to Reformed churches in France and other parts of Western Europe.

In the final years of his life Calvin struggled with an array of painful illnesses that often confined him to his bed. In February 1564 he delivered his final lecture and his last sermon. On April 25 he dictated his will and two days later received a farewell visit from the members of the Little Council. He met for the last time with the other ministers on May 19 and died in his home on May 27, 1564. The following day he was buried in a common cemetery, according to Beza, "with no extraordinary pomp, and, as he had commanded, without any grave-stone."[21] No theologian's life perfectly coheres with his or her theology, but there is something fitting about Calvin's wish that his grave not become a memorial and that all human praise be given to God.

Questions

1. Calvin says little explicitly about his personal religious development, and historians have been unable to pinpoint exactly when he was no longer obedient to Rome and had become fully committed to the movement for the reform of the church. Does that mean that Calvin did not have a "conversion"? What is a religious conversion? Is there only one kind of conversion or are there many? What was Calvin's conversion?

2. One of the significant differences between theologians like Calvin and other Protestant Reformers of the sixteenth century and theologians today is that very few of the latter write commentaries on the Bible. Why do so few contemporary theologians write biblical commentaries, and how, as a result, does their theology differ from their sixteenth-century predecessors?

3. Calvin's efforts to reform both the church and the public life of Geneva will seem strange to many readers today. Clearly Calvin had not heard about religious pluralism or even the separation of church and state! Does that mean that Calvin is irrelevant for Christians who live today in religiously and culturally diverse communities?

CHAPTER TWO

THE KNOWLEDGE OF GOD

I s there a theological theme or doctrine that is at the center of Calvin's theology and gives it its coherence? That question has been much discussed in Calvin scholarship. It is a question asked not only of Calvin but also of any theologian who writes a "systematic theology"—that is, any attempt to describe the coherence of Christian faith—because it often provides a way to clarify and organize the theological proposal. Is "justification by faith," for example, the theological center to Martin Luther's description of Christian faith? Is God's self-revelation in Jesus Christ the center to Karl Barth's theology? Calvin does indeed claim that justification is "the main hinge on which religion turns," and he does argue that Jesus Christ is the central teaching of the Bible, but are either of these themes the center or organizing principle in his theology?

If there is a single theological conviction or organizing center to Calvin's theology, there certainly is no consensus among Calvin scholars as to what it is. François Wendel, for example, argues that "the idea that dominates the whole of Calvin's theological exposition" is that God and humanity "must be seen in their rightful places," and that is "the infinite distance separating God from his creature . . . the radical distinction between the Divine and the human."[1] On the other hand, Wendel also acknowledges that for Calvin "the aim of all study of the Scriptures must be the Christ."[2] Obviously these two claims are closely related, but they are not the same. A good case can be made that both of these convictions are central to Calvin's theology, which in turn raises the question of whether there is a single center to Calvin's theology or multiple "central themes."[3]

What Is the Knowledge of God?

One theme frequently proposed as the center or organizing principle of Calvin's theology is the knowledge of God.[4] The first Latin edition (1536) of the *Institutes* (the *Institution of the Christian Religion*) begins with the sentence, "Nearly the whole of sacred doctrine consists in these two parts: knowledge of God and of ourselves."[5] Twenty-three years later the final edition of the *Institutes* begins with the sentence, "Nearly all the wisdom we possess, that is to say, true and sound wisdom, consists of two parts: the knowledge of God and of ourselves. But while joined by many bonds, which one precedes and brings forth the other is not easy to discern."[6] "Sacred doctrine" in the 1536 edition has been replaced in 1559 by "wisdom," but the description of the goal as "knowledge of God and of ourselves" remains the same.

Not only is the knowledge of God a prominent theme in what Calvin wrote, but it was also what Calvin promoted in Geneva and Strasbourg. The knowledge of God was not just a theological concept for him, but something to which he gave significant time and energy. As we have seen, the *Articles Concerning the Organization of the Church and of Worship at Geneva*, which he wrote in 1537 at the beginning of his first stay in Geneva, emphasized the importance of instructing children in Christian faith. To that end he wrote the *Instruction in Faith* of 1537, and when he returned to Geneva in 1541 for the second and final time, he drafted the *Ecclesiastical Ordinances*, which called for children to be instructed in a catechism. Once again Calvin provided the means of instruction—the *Geneva Catechism* of 1545. The *Ecclesiastical Ordinances* also called for the creation of a college to educate youth in languages and the humanities in preparation for both the ministry and for civil government. It took Calvin several years to realize that goal, but finally in June 1559, five years before his death, the Genevan academy was opened. Calvin lived what he wrote and proclaimed. His life was given to the advancement of the knowledge of God.

Several important questions surround this theme of the knowledge of God in Calvin's theology. What kind of knowledge did he have in mind? What is the relation between this knowledge and faith? Does everyone have this knowledge?

First, what kind of knowledge is this? Calvin described it in two ways. Knowledge of God is inseparably related to self-knowledge. In both the first and last editions of the *Institutes*, Calvin distinguishes, but does not separate, these two forms of knowledge. Although not the same, they are also inseparable and are so closely related that Calvin acknowledges it is difficult to determine which comes first. In the opening sentences of the 1559 edition Calvin writes, "no one can look upon himself without immediately turning his thoughts to the contemplation of God, in whom he 'lives and moves' [Acts 17:28]."[7] At the same time a person "never achieves a clear knowledge of himself unless he has first looked upon God's face, and then descends from contemplating him to scrutinize himself."[8] So, where then does one begin? Should we begin not with human beings but with God, because if we begin with ourselves we risk turning God into a projection of human aspirations and ideals? Or should we begin with ourselves, with the human longing for that which transcends human finitude? "The order of right teaching," Calvin argues, "requires that we discuss the former [knowledge of God] first, then proceed afterward to treat the latter [knowledge of ourselves]."[9] The order of "right teaching," however, is not necessarily the same thing as the order in which knowledge of God is experienced.

True knowledge of God is not simply information about God. It is not so much knowledge *about* God as it is knowledge *of* God—that is, experiential knowledge, knowledge that bears directly on one's self-understanding, knowledge that involves the heart just as much as it does the mind. It is not simply knowledge that God is or that God exists. Calvin does not begin the *Institutes* by presenting "proofs" or arguments for the existence of God; he simply assumes God's existence because it is "beyond controversy" that in every human mind there is "an awareness of divinity" or a "seed of religion."[10] Those who ask, "What is God?" ask the wrong question. They are only engaging in idle (and perhaps idol) speculation. True knowledge of God is not just knowledge that God is. What good is that, asks Calvin? To truly know God is "to grasp what befits us and is proper to his glory, in fine, what is to our advantage to know of him."[11] Knowledge of God, therefore, differs from other kinds of knowledge in that it is "beneficial." It has a practical utility that serves two purposes: it teaches fear and reverence of God (what is "proper to his glory") and it teaches that we "should learn to seek every good from him, and, having received it, to credit it to his account."[12] True knowledge of God is inseparable from the self-understanding of the knower. One cannot have knowledge of God without that knowledge bearing directly on how one understands one's self. And one cannot properly understand one's self apart from knowing God.

The kind of knowledge Calvin is describing might not be well received today in many colleges and universities. And Calvin would probably consider the description of human beings given by most social science departments (such as psychology, sociology, and anthropology) and some physical science departments (such as biology) a seriously flawed reductionism. They tell us something important about what it means to be human, but separately and even collectively they are incomplete and inadequate because they omit the most important thing about human beings—that human beings are constituted by the fact that they are known by God, are enabled to know God and to live before God in fear, reverence, love, and gratitude. Knowledge about God, therefore, is an utterly different kind of knowledge than "factual" or "objective" knowledge. One cannot truly know God without loving God and living before God obediently and thankfully.

God the Creator and God the Redeemer

In addition to the distinction between knowledge of God and self-knowledge, there is another twofold knowledge of God—the knowledge of God the creator and the knowledge of God the redeemer. In the *Institutes* Calvin refers to knowledge of God the creator as "the primal and simple knowledge to which the very order of nature would have led us if Adam had remained upright."[13] This is not the knowledge of God Christians have in Jesus Christ the mediator, the knowledge of God the redeemer. The difference is that only the latter, the knowledge of God the redeemer, is "saving" knowledge. The former, knowledge of God the creator, refers to what can be known about God in creation and in the Bible; "as much in the fashioning of the universe as in the general teaching of Scripture the Lord shows himself simply to be the Creator."[14]

Furthermore, Calvin tells the reader "we shall now discuss the first aspect (God the creator); the second (God the redeemer) will be dealt with in its proper place." That comment has raised two questions. First, where precisely in the *Institutes* does Calvin's discussion of God the Creator begin and end, and what is the "proper place" where Calvin discusses knowledge of God the Redeemer? The second, related point concerns this twofold knowledge itself. Does this theme provide the structure for the *Institutes*, especially the final edition of 1559? If so, what are we to make of Calvin's division of the *Institutes* into four books, apparently reflecting the structure of the Apostles' Creed? Is the basic structure of the *Institutes* the twofold knowledge of God (God the creator in Book I and God the redeemer in Books II–IV), or is it the fourfold division of the Apostles' Creed? Or are the two—the twofold knowledge of God and the fourfold division of the Apostles' Creed—somehow compatible?[15]

Calvin begins his discussion of God the Redeemer in Book II of the *Institutes*, following his discussion of sin, and continues it through Book III, how the Spirit enables Christians to receive the benefits of Christ, and Book IV, the church and the external means of grace. The topic in Book I, however, is, in the words of the Apostles' Creed, the knowledge of "God the Father almighty, maker of heaven and earth," who "supports us by his power, governs us by his providence, nourishes us by his goodness, and attends us with all sorts of blessings."[16] Obviously, these two forms of knowledge cannot be permanently separated from one another because the one triune God is both creator and redeemer, but one knows God as creator differently than one knows God as redeemer. Or, as Calvin puts it in discussing the subject matter of the Bible, there is, first, "that kind of knowledge by which one is permitted to grasp who that God is who founded and governs the universe," and, second, there is that "inner" knowledge "which alone quickens dead souls, whereby God is known not only as the Founder of the universe and the sole Author and Ruler of all that is made, but also in the person of the Mediator as the Redeemer."[17] Both these forms of knowledge of God are reciprocally related to knowledge of self. One only knows oneself truly and fully when one knows oneself in relation to the one triune God who is Creator, Redeemer, and Sustainer.

The knowledge of God involves the mind or intellect, but it is above all else a knowing that involves the heart because God is not known "where there is no religion or piety," and by piety Calvin means "that reverence joined with love of God which the knowledge of his benefits induces."[18] Knowledge of God involves both the mind and the heart, and what Christians know are the "benefits" of God's grace in Jesus Christ, benefits that evoke reverence, worship, love, and gratitude. Calvin's seal was an outstretched hand holding a burning heart, yet another indication that the primary influence on Calvin among the teachers of the early church was Augustine.[19]

One of the distinctive features of this knowledge of God is that it is inseparable from faith, which Calvin describes as "the principal work of the Holy Spirit" and defines as "a firm and certain knowledge of God's benevolence toward us, founded upon the truth of the freely given promise in Christ, both revealed to our minds and sealed upon our hearts through the Holy Spirit."[20] Faith, therefore, entails knowledge. It has content and is not sheer ecstatic experience. It is a "firm and certain knowledge of God's benevolence" (to which we will return when we discuss Calvin's understanding of God in chapter 4). The basis or foundation for this knowledge of God is God's freely given promise in Jesus Christ (to which we shall return in chapter 5). And the means by which one knows God's benevolence in Jesus Christ is the work of the Holy Spirit (the topic in chapters 6 and 7). It is the Holy Spirit who reveals to the mind and seals upon the heart this knowledge of God.

Revealed Knowledge and Natural Knowledge of God

Calvin did not think people can reason their way to God. We often think of knowledge as something we can discover and acquire by means of reason. Reason, especially what we sometimes refer to as "scientific" reason, is the "instrument" by which we uncover or discover information or "engineer" new knowledge about reality. From this perspective it is the rational scientist who acquires knowledge and who is the primary agent, the one who does the knowing, and it is "objective reality" that is uncovered and then known. Calvin's understanding of the knowledge of God is quite different. It is God and not the individual self who is the primary agent in the process of knowing.

The individual self is not so much the subject, the primary agent, the one who "discovers" God, as the one who is first known and only by being known by God is enabled to know both the one by whom one is known and one's self as well. When the self knows God, the self is not so much the knower, the active initiator, as the passive recipient, the one who is known. Knowledge of God, therefore, is not discovered but revealed and received. Such knowledge, as Calvin puts it in his definition of faith, is "revealed to the mind and sealed upon our hearts through the Holy Spirit." It is the Spirit and not the self who is the primary agent when it comes to knowledge of God, a knowledge that is both "revealed" or unveiled to the mind by the Spirit and sealed upon the heart in such a manner that what (or who) is known is also loved with all of one's mind and soul and strength. This knowledge then is not so much an accomplishment or achievement as it is a generous gift of God's grace to which the only appropriate response is gratitude and doxology.

The knowledge of God, as Calvin understands it, refers both to knowledge of God the creator and God the redeemer. As we have seen, two features of this knowledge are particularly important. First, this knowledge is not so much something acquired as it is graciously given. It cannot be grasped but only gratefully received. And, second, this knowledge is "useful" or "beneficial" in that it has to do with the redemption, the healing, of those who have been blind and have lost their way.

Does this mean that for Calvin there is no knowledge of God other than revealed knowledge? Calvin points to three places where God's glory can be seen in the world. First, God has revealed God's self and "daily discloses himself in the whole workmanship of the universe."[21] God is disclosed in the macrocosm of the order and structure of the universe, which is "a sort of mirror in which we can contemplate God, who is otherwise, invisible."[22] Second, God is evident in the microcosm of the human being, "because he is a rare example of God's power, goodness, and wisdom, and contains within himself enough miracles to occupy our minds."[23] Human beings are both a workshop "graced with God's unnumbered works" and a storehouse "overflowing with inestimable riches," which should evoke from humans nothing except doxology.[24] Third, human history testifies to the providence of God—God's clemency to the godly and God's severity to the wicked. God's care for the poor and the lost is a "proof" of heavenly providence and of God's "fatherly kindness." But if there is, as Calvin puts it, no spot in the universe and no place in human history that does not declare the glory of God, why are human beings unable to know God and why must knowledge of God be given to them, revealed to them by the Holy Spirit?

Here Calvin follows the apostle Paul's argument in the first chapter of Romans. The universe is full of "burning lamps" that shine forth the glory of God, but humans cannot see them. Blinded by sin they are unable to see what is there in front of them. The problem is not with God but with sin that leaves humans both blinded and also without excuse. "The heavens are telling the glory of God; and the firmament proclaims his handiwork" (Ps. 19:1). Creation witnesses to the glory of God, but sinful human beings cannot discern what nature proclaims. In his commentary on Romans 1:18-23, Calvin argues that although God's majesty shines forth in all his works, that is of no use to people who are blinded by their sin. "But we are not so blind that we can plead ignorance without being convicted of perversity."[25]

Not all theologians agree as to what Calvin meant by his claim that there is "a seed of religion" in all human beings, that "a sense of divinity which can never be effaced is engraved" upon all minds. All human beings are imbued with a firm conviction about God "from which the inclination toward religion springs as from a seed,"[26] but what is the status of this "natural" knowledge of God? Does it serve only a negative purpose? That is, are human beings so blinded by their sinful pride that this knowledge, this sense of divinity, this inclination toward religion, only leads them to idolatry and only serves to leave them without excuse before God's judgment? Or does this "sense of divinity" play a positive role in the development of Christian faith? Does this "inclination toward religion" point to something in the structure of human beings that enables them to receive what the Holy Spirit reveals to their minds and seals upon their hearts?

In 1934 two prominent Swiss Reformed theologians—Karl Barth and Emil Brunner—debated the question of "natural theology." Is the only true knowledge of God revealed knowledge or are there some things about God that can be known by reason and by the observation of nature? Because of the historical circumstances, this was no mere "academic" debate. Adolf Hitler and the National Socialists had recently come to power in Germany. A small number of church leaders gathered at Barmen in May, 1934, and issued the Theological Declaration of Barmen that rejected the attempt by the German-Christian church to blend the gospel with an ideology that celebrated the German people and Aryan racial supremacy. It was in this highly charged political atmosphere that Emil Brunner, professor of theology in Zürich, published an essay that responded to criticisms Barth had previously made of his interpretation and use of natural theology (*theologia naturalis*).

The central issue was whether a "natural theology" based on the image of God, the *imago dei*, in human beings is possible. Brunner appealed both to Scripture and to John Calvin. He drew a distinction between a formal and a material understanding of the *imago*, affirmed a double revelation—in creation and in Christ—and argued for the reality of preserving or general grace, by which he meant "the manner in which God is present to his fallen creature."[27] If there is not some sense of God's preserving grace in creation, some "point of contact" between God and humanity, then human beings would be unable to receive God's grace because the Word of God "could not reach a man who had lost his consciousness of God entirely."[28] The church can proclaim the gospel, Brunner argued, only because there is a remnant of the image of God in sinful humanity. This remnant is humanity's "undestroyed formal likeness to God," and it is "the objective possibility of the revelation of God in his 'Word.'" Apart from this "point of contact" between humanity and God the church's proclamation would be unintelligible. Furthermore, Brunner insisted, this was also Calvin's position.

Barth's response was an angry *No! Answer to Emil Brunner*. He rejected both Brunner's summary of Barth's position and Brunner's attempt to clarify what he meant by "natural theology." The latter, Barth wrote, is "every (positive *or* negative) *formulation of a system* which claims to be theological, i.e., to interpret divine revelation, whose *subject*, however, differs fundamentally from the revelation in Jesus Christ and whose *method* therefore differs equally from the exposition of Holy Scripture."[29] Within what Barth described as "real theology" natural theology does not exist and as such is not a separate topic. The appropriate response to natural theology should be to "hit it and kill it as soon as you see it," just as one would a serpent. Furthermore, Barth sharply disagreed with Brunner's interpretation of Calvin. As Barth read him, Calvin's position on natural knowledge of God was derived from Paul, beginning in Romans 1:19. Hence Calvin did not believe there is "a capacity which man has retained and which has to be reconstituted by faith, as a point of contact for revelation and for the new life in Christ." Concerning Brunner's interpretation of Calvin, Barth concludes, "the whole process is enough to make one weep."[30]

Questions

1. Calvin argues that God is not known where there is no piety ("reverence joined with love of God which the knowledge of his benefits induces"). Do you agree with him?

2. Barth and Brunner read Calvin in drastically different ways. Between these two "heirs of Calvin" who had the better interpretation of him? Is there "a point of contact" between God and the world that enables humans to know something about God? Or is the only knowledge about God God's miracle of self-revelation in Jesus Christ?

3. If there is "a sense of divinity" in all people, does this provide sufficient "common ground" for discussion about God among the world's different religions?

CHAPTER THREE

A LAMP AND A MIRROR

Although the structure and beauty of the world are like burning lamps that "show forth the glory of its author" and "bathe us wholly in their radiance," and even though they may "strike some sparks,"[1] human beings cannot know God the redeemer by contemplating the world or themselves. Even worse, because all humans have a seed of religion, an awareness of God, within them, they "fly off into empty speculations," and imagine God "as they have fashioned him in their own presumption."[2] Indeed, "scarcely a single person has ever been found who did not fashion for himself an idol or specter in place of God."[3] Left to its own devices humanity's knowledge of God is finally confusion, superstition, error, and idolatry.

Near-Sightedness, Self-Deception, and the Spectacles of Scripture

Like the Bible he studied so carefully, Calvin uses several metaphors to describe the abyss of human sin. Because of their sin humans are stupid, dull, confused, asleep, and blind. Sinful people cannot see the truth that is in front of their noses. They are "bleary-eyed" people with weak vision. When shown a beautiful book—for example, the book of nature—they may be able to discern it is a book with writing in it, yet they "can scarcely construe two words."[4] Calvin's use of the term "bleary-eyed" describes the experience of some nearsighted people when they were children and before their condition was diagnosed by an ophthalmologist. They believed that the world or reality was what their eyes showed them, and some report being shocked when as children they received their first pair of glasses and discovered that trees were not just undifferentiated green objects but made up of leaves. Reality turned out to be decidedly different from what they had perceived it to be.

The same is true, Calvin argues, for human beings whose ability to see what is directly in front of them, either in the natural world or in their personal experience, is distorted by their sinfulness. Their "astigmatism" is their sin, and, because one feature of sin is its capacity for self-deception, nearsighted people often do not know they are nearsighted until the ophthalmologist gives them "corrective lenses" and enables them to see the world and themselves differently. Where the metaphor of nearsightedness "breaks down" or is inadequate is that it describes the human dilemma only as an inability to perceive correctly the world "out there." In fact, our distorted vision describes not only our inability to discern the truth about the world "out there," but also our inability to discern the truth "within"—the truth about ourselves as well. In the words of 1 John 1:8, "If we say that we have no sin, we deceive ourselves, and the truth is not in us."

Nearsightedness or self-deception is a vicious circle, an abyss, from which we are unable to extricate ourselves. Because our knowledge is limited to what we can see, we are dependent on a physician, an ophthalmologist, to do for us what we cannot do for ourselves. So too, Calvin argues, God does for us what we cannot do for ourselves by giving us "the aid of spectacles." With the corrective lenses of Scripture, God accommodates God's self to our "disability" so that "we will begin to read distinctly," and then Scripture "gathering up the otherwise confused knowledge of God in our minds, having dispersed our dullness,"[5] will show us clearly who God is.

The Bible is "a special gift" from God to the world in which God gives the world something better than the best human wisdom can provide; "however much froward men try to gnaw at it, nevertheless it clearly is crammed with thoughts that could not be humanly conceived."[6] In the Bible, "God, to instruct the church, not merely uses mute teachers but also opens his most hallowed lips."[7] The Bible is something more than an important religious text, written by devout authors. It is a means of grace that has its origin not in human wisdom but in God's "singular providence." It is the means by which God extricates humans from their stupidity, confusion, and blindness (or at least their severe nearsightedness), and enables them to know the truth about God, the world, and themselves. It is indispensable, not because there is something magical about it, but because in it Christians are to "reverently embrace what it pleases God there to witness of himself."[8] Consequently, "in order that true religion may shine upon us, we ought to hold that it must take its beginning from heavenly doctrine and that no one can get even the slightest taste of right and sound doctrine unless he be a pupil of Scripture."[9]

For Calvin, "true religion" is found first and foremost in Scripture, and then by means of it what is true can be discerned in the church's creeds, history, teaching, and religious customs, and other forms of human wisdom. Calvin valued the tools he had learned from humanism for the interpretation of texts, including the Bible, and he also had great respect and appreciation for those who preceded him in the never-ending task of biblical interpretation (especially Augustine, Chrysostom, Jerome, and Bernard of Clairvaux), but like many other sixteenth-century Reformers Calvin rejected as a "pernicious error" the notion that the authority of Scripture depends upon the consent of the church. The Bible does not receive its authority from the church; rather, the church is founded upon the writings of the prophets and the preaching of the apostles.

Because the Bible is central and indispensable to Christian faith, every Christian must be a "pupil of Scripture"—not just in the religious education given to youth, which Calvin understood to be a primary responsibility of the church, but throughout the rest of life as well. It is not just the leaders of the church who are to be lifelong students of Scripture, but those who sit in the pews as well. The call to be a pupil of Scripture was for Calvin not simply a theological affirmation of "the authority of Scripture" but a commitment he lived—not only by preaching several times a week, but by lecturing on Scripture, participating in discussions of it with his fellow ministers, and for the last half of his life, from 1540 until his death, writing commentaries on many of the books of the Bible. Like Luther, Melanchthon, Bucer, and many other sixteenth-century Reformers, Calvin's commitment to the study of Scripture was something he both believed and practiced, working on his commentaries in his bed even when beset by illness and pain.

An Accommodating Spirit

Christians must be pupils of Scripture because "God is its Author" and "God in person speaks in it."[10] By itself, however, reason alone cannot convince anyone that the Bible is true—"true" not only in what it says about God but true in the sense that it is "good news" for the one who reads it. Rational proof simply cannot provide that conviction. Because the Bible is a means of grace, its truth can be known only by what Calvin describes as "the secret testimony of the Spirit." Faith requires more than intellectual conviction. Because faith is as much a matter of the heart as the mind, the knowledge that piety requires is dependent not on reason but on the testimony of the Spirit. Hence, "the Word will not find acceptance in men's hearts before it is sealed by the inward testimony of the Spirit."[11] Remember Calvin's definition of faith: "a firm and certain knowledge of God's benevolence toward us, founded upon the truth of the freely given promise in Christ, *both revealed to our mind and sealed upon our hearts through the Holy Spirit*." The Bible contains what Calvin refers to as "right and sound doctrine," but what the Bible teaches becomes "efficacious" only when the Spirit enables the mind to know what it cannot know by itself and only when the Spirit seals that knowledge upon the heart.

The Bible is a means of grace because both the knowledge it offers and the conviction that it is true are not available to human inquiry and discovery. As a scholar of Renaissance humanism, Calvin knew the importance of discerning the intention of a text's author, but as a Christian theologian he also knew that the teaching of Scripture is not finally available and certainly not convincing or efficacious (that is, will not find acceptance by the reader) apart from the work of the Spirit. In other words, in so far as anyone—a theologically educated minister or the least educated person in the pew—hears the truth of the gospel in a biblical text, that is not an achievement of human wisdom or the result of an acquired skill (not even three years of theological education, including Hebrew and Greek!) but a gracious gift of the Spirit.

Calvin's emphasis on the necessity of the work of the Spirit in order to hear the truth of the gospel led him to an important hermeneutical and theological principle that had far-reaching implications: while God's Word and the Holy Spirit are distinct realities they are also inseparable. That means that the Word of God in any biblical text is "ineffective" apart from the activity of the Spirit; "the Word will not find acceptance in men's hearts before it is sealed by the inward testimony of the Spirit." Apart from the Spirit a biblical text will remain only words and not the Word in the words.

The other side of the coin is that the Spirit must not be separated from the Word, as do "certain giddy men" who "with great haughtiness exalting the teaching office of the Spirit, despise all reading and laugh at the simplicity of those who, as they express it, still follow the dead and killing letter."[12] In a 1545 treatise, *Against the Fantastic and Furious Sect of the Libertines Who Are Called "Spiritual,"* Calvin attacked Quintin of Hainaut and his followers (Quintinists), who had infiltrated the court of Marguerite of Angoulême. These mystical spiritualists, according to Calvin, wanted "to change Scripture into allegories and to long for a better and more perfect wisdom than we find in it."[13] In emphasizing the Spirit and denigrating Scripture the libertines "lead us beyond the limits of Scripture to the end that each might follow his own interests and the devil's illusions instead of following the truth of God."[14] Rather than relying only on the text or only on the inspiration of the Spirit, Christians should hold to "the pure and plain Word of God where He has clearly revealed His Word to us" and "pray that by His Holy Spirit He will want to implant it in our hearts."[15] The Word without the Spirit is mere information and neither transformative nor redemptive; and the Spirit without the Word invites self-deception and idolatry.[16]

God's Spirit reveals the gospel and seals (or makes efficacious) its promises on an individual's heart. God does so by "accommodating" God's self to the Bible, just as God has accommodated God's self to a sinful world in the person of Jesus Christ. God's majesty is "too lofty to be attained by mortal men, who are like grubs crawling upon the earth"; and, in agreement with Irenaeus, Calvin describes the Father, who is himself infinite and as such beyond human comprehension, as one who makes himself known in the Son, thereby accommodating himself "to our little measure lest our minds be overwhelmed by the immensity of his glory."[17] Calvin compares God to nurses who speak to children by lisping; "such forms of speaking do not so much express clearly what God is like as accommodate the knowledge of him to our slight capacity."[18] God's Word becomes flesh in the person of Jesus of Nazareth, who alone is truly human and who is God's "accommodation" to finite, sinful people. In his commentary on 1 Peter 1:20, Calvin insists that we cannot believe in God except through Christ "in whom God in a manner makes Himself little . . . in order to accommodate Himself to our comprehension . . . and it is Christ alone who can make our consciences at peace, so that we may dare to come in confidence to God."[19] God makes God's self known in and by means of his Word—his Word incarnate in Jesus of Nazareth and his Word written in the Bible.

Gospel and Law

Calvin believed it was "perfectly clear" in the moral law and the prophets that Jesus Christ is the "end"—in the sense of fulfillment and not as replacement—of the law, and that "apart from Christ the saving knowledge of God does not stand." But because God's covenantal promises are fulfilled in Jesus Christ, he cannot be understood apart from the moral law. The fulfillment must not be separated from the promise. So too if Christians look only upon the law, they "can only be despondent, confused, and despairing in mind" because God's law exposes the sinfulness of all people.[20] Just as Word and Spirit are reciprocally related, so too are gospel and law.

Calvin's discussion of the relation between law and gospel is important for understanding his interpretation of the authority of Scripture. The law has not one but three "uses" or functions. First, it "shows" the righteousness God expects from humans and in so doing compels sinners to recognize their unrighteousness. In this sense, the law—indeed Scripture itself—is "like a mirror." "In it we contemplate our weakness, then the iniquity arising from this, and finally the curse coming from both—just as a mirror shows us the spots on our face."[21] What people see in the mirror of the law is how far they fall short of the expectations of the covenant. They are anything but God's righteous and faithful creatures. What they discover in the mirror, however, should not drive them to despair, but should make them flee to God's mercy in Christ, "repose entirely in it, hide deep within it, and seize upon it alone for righteousness and merit."[22]

Second, the law serves as a deterrent in the community to those "who are untouched by any care for what is just and right unless compelled by hearing the dire threats in the law."[23] The restraint of the wicked does not make them righteous before God because they do not voluntarily obey but are restrained in their evil only by fear of what the law threatens. Although some Christians today continue to argue that the Ten Commandments should be placed in every courtroom in the United States, not many people believe those who "are untouched" by what is just and right would be deterred.

The third use of the law is for Calvin its principal and proper purpose. Among those in whom the Spirit is at work—revealing the promises of the covenant to their minds and sealing them upon their hearts—the law serves an indispensable pedagogical purpose. The law enables them to "learn more thoroughly each day the nature of the Lord's will." For every Christian the task of growing in the knowledge of God's will is never finished, but is one that must be taken up anew each day, which is another reason Calvin insists every Christian must be a lifelong pupil of Scripture. The task is unfinished not simply because of the limitations of human knowledge but because the God Calvin discovers in Scripture is a living God who continues to do new things in the world and to call God's people to new and surprising forms of obedience.

In addition, Christians are called not only to grow in their knowledge of God's will, but by "frequent meditation upon it to be aroused to obedience, be strengthened in it, and be drawn back from the slippery path of transgression."[24] To explain what he means, Calvin refers to "innumerable texts" in Psalm 119, especially to verse 105, "Your word is a lamp to my feet and a light to my path." The law does indeed instruct, but the point of its instruction is "a readiness to obey." The law does indict, convict, and restrain, but most importantly, when read in the power of the Spirit, it regenerates and transforms by illuminating the path Christians should walk. Calvin's frequent use of metaphors like "the path" and "the way" describes not only the use of the law and the role of the Bible but his larger sense of the nature of the Christian life (as we shall see in chapter 6); "for the LORD watches over the way of the righteous, but the way of the wicked will perish" (Ps. 1:6).

The Authority of Scripture

The three uses or purposes of the law demonstrate not only Calvin's understanding of the relation between the gospel and the law but also his interpretation of the authority of Scripture. The latter has been a much discussed and debated issue, especially in nineteenth- and twentieth-century Protestant theology. In response to the emergence of historical criticism and the issues it has raised for biblical interpretation, some theologians have argued that the "authority" or normative status of Scripture is its inerrancy and divine origin. For example, theologians at Princeton Seminary in the last half of the nineteenth century argued that the Bible, at least in its "original manuscripts" (those not marred by mistakes in transmission), was "without error" because it was "authored" by God and dictated by God to human authors who were inspired by the Holy Spirit. Theologians who argue for some version of this interpretation of the authority of the Bible often appeal to the first chapter of the Westminster Confession of Faith of 1647, which affirms that God, who is truth itself, is the author of Scripture, although it is the Holy Spirit that assures one of the Bible's "infallible truth."[25] Many of these same theologians also argue that this is not only the position of the Westminster Confession of Faith but Calvin's as well. The extent to which the Westminster Confession reflects Calvin's interpretation of the authority of the Bible has been much debated during the last two hundred years.

Calvin clearly believed that God is the "author" of the Bible, but what did he mean by that and is it God's "authorship" that makes the Bible authoritative for Christians? There are certainly many texts in the *Institutes* and in his biblical commentaries where Calvin describes the "authority" of the Bible in language that lends itself to this interpretation. In the Bible God "opens his own most hallowed lips," God put into the minds of the patriarchs of the Old Testament "what they should then hand down to their posterity," and God engraved on their hearts the "firm certainty of doctrine."[26] Furthermore, people correctly understand the authority of the Bible only when they regard it "as having sprung from heaven, as if there the living words of God were heard."[27] In his commentary on 2 Timothy 3:16, a text that dominated many of the debates in the nineteenth and twentieth centuries, Calvin describes the writers of the Bible as instruments or organs through whom doctrine is dictated by the Holy Spirit. Some theologians, especially those in the so-called evangelical tradition, have argued that the position taken in the first chapter of the Westminster Confession of Faith and that later taken by Princeton theologians concerning the inerrancy of the lost autographs of the Bible are simply restatements of Calvin's position on biblical authority.

On the other hand, if we return to Calvin's description of faith it is clear that the foundation for Christian faith is not the Bible but "the truth of the freely given promise in Christ." To be sure, Calvin believed that the truth of that promise is found in the Bible. The theological issue, however, long disputed among Calvin's followers, has been the precise relationship between the Bible as God's Word and Jesus Christ as God's Word. Are these the same thing or are they different senses of God's Word? Is believing in Christ the same thing as believing in the Bible? And which side of the debate would Calvin have favored? That is not an easy issue to answer unequivocally, because it forces Calvin to address questions he did not ask, questions that have emerged in a different historical era and theological context than that of the sixteenth century. This discussion is also unfortunate because it poses the issue primarily in terms of what Calvin did and did not say about Scripture. A good case can be made that far more important than what Calvin said about Scripture is how he used it and the role it actually played in his ministry in Geneva. What Calvin thought about Scripture is perhaps best understood in terms of the time and energy he gave to preaching from it and lecturing and teaching about it. He was far more concerned that the Bible be taught and proclaimed, that Christians be "pupils of Scripture" every day of their lives, that the Bible be their teacher, the lamp unto their paths through life, than that they say the right things about it. Like Luther and many of the other Reformers, Calvin differs from many "modern" (post-Enlightenment) theologians not primarily in what he said about the Bible, but in the indispensable role the Bible played in his understanding of Christian faith and theology.

Questions

1. One way to think about the authority of the Bible is to distinguish between what the Bible is and what it does or its function in the church and in Christian life. Is the Bible authoritative because of what it is—for example, that it is inspired by God—or is it authoritative because of its unique and indispensable role as the witness to Jesus Christ?

2. Is God's law a good thing or a bad thing? Paul writes that the gospel frees Christians from the law. But if Christians are free from the law why does Calvin claim that Christians should embrace the law and live according to it?

3. If Calvin thinks Christians cannot hear the gospel in the words of Scripture unless God's Spirit enables them to do so, doesn't that mean that religious experience rather than the Bible is the true authority for Christian faith?

CHAPTER FOUR

GOD'S GOOD WILL

I f the Bible provides finite, sinful people "true and sound wisdom," what does the Bible say about God? The "most perfect way of seeking God," Calvin argues, is not "empty speculation" that "merely flits in the brain." We should not attempt with "bold curiosity" to investigate God's essence, because the splendor of God, as Calvin describes it, is "an inexplicable labyrinth" that leads human beings in their reason and imagination to substitute images and idols for the glory of God. The result is human opinion, superstition, and finally idolatry rather than what Calvin describes as "true and sound wisdom." The latter is true religion and it is to be found in God's Word, "where God is truly and vividly described to us from his works." It is better, Calvin advises, "to limp along this path" in pursuit of God by becoming "a pupil of Scripture" than "to dash with all speed outside it" by constructing images of God that satisfy human needs.[1]

God's Triunity

What we learn from the Bible's description of God's "works" or activity in the world is first and foremost that God is triune. Like most other sixteenth-century Reformers, Calvin's quarrel with the Catholic Church was not about the classical doctrines of the Trinity and Christology. He affirmed the description of Christian faith in the ecumenical councils of the early church. God's "work" in the world is above all else Jesus Christ, God's Word "endued with flesh." "The very hypostasis that shines forth in the Son is in the Father" and the same is true of the Holy Spirit.[2] Both the Word incarnate in Jesus and the Holy Spirit are God, and yet each is "to be thought of as other than the Father."[3] The three "persons" are distinct and not to be confused with one another but also inseparable. Calvin thought it squeamish and obstinate to quarrel over whether the Greek term *hypostasis* or the Latin *persona* best describes the threeness in the triune life. The threeness is not a distinction of essence ("since the essence of God is simple and undivided"[4]), and Greek and Latin Christians agree on what is truly important—namely, "our conviction that three are spoken of, each of which is entirely God, yet that there is not more than one God."[5] In describing the threeness of God Calvin preferred the term "subsistence" to "person," but insisted that subsistence is different from essence. The Trinity is not an affirmation of three gods. The name God "pertains no less to the Son and the Spirit than to the Father," and there is among the three subsistences a unity of essence.[6] He emphatically denied that the name God "applies to the Father alone"; "under the name of God is understood a single, simple essence, in which we comprehend three persons or hypostases."[7]

God's Gracious Good Will

In keeping with his claim that one should avoid empty speculation about the essence of God, Calvin describes the triune God on the basis of God's "work" or "acts" of creation and redemption. It is when we examine God's six days of creation that we are led to "God's fatherly love toward mankind."[8] While Calvin has much to say about God's love for the world in Jesus Christ, the primary metaphor by which he describes God is that of God's will. Faith is a firm and certain knowledge of God, but it is not simply knowledge that God is, that God exists, but knowledge that is inseparable from God's Word. What faith knows about God on the basis of God's Word—that is, on the basis of Jesus Christ—is God's good will. "Faith," Calvin writes, "is not merely a question of knowing that God exists, but also—and this especially—of knowing what his will is toward us. *For it is not so much our concern to know who he is in himself, as what he wills to be toward us.*"[9]

At the heart of Calvin's understanding of God is God's good will to sinners in the person of Jesus Christ. Consequently, what Christians know about God's will on the basis of Jesus Christ is above all else that God wills them good—and God's good will is the promise of grace which assures them of God's mercy, a mercy that is freely given. It is given not to people who are good and righteous but to sinners who are lost and unable to find their way back to life before God. This grace and mercy are given unconditionally, with no strings attached. It is on this freely given promise that faith rests. Hence Christian faith is not faith in faith itself (what is sometimes described as "fideism"), not faith that trusts in faith itself (because human faith is beset by doubts), but faith that has a firm foundation in God's promise in Jesus Christ. In one of the more lyrical passages of the *Institutes*, Calvin writes:

> Faith is certain that God is true in all things, whether he command or forbid, whether he promise or threaten; and it also obediently receives his commandments, observes his prohibitions, heeds his threats. Nevertheless, faith properly begins with the promise, rests in it, and ends in it. For in God faith seeks life: a life that is not found in commandments or declarations of penalties, but in the promise of mercy, and only in a freely given promise.[10]

Particularly important is Calvin's repeated use of the expression "freely given promise." He describes the Christian life in terms of gratitude and doxology—gratitude because new life in Jesus Christ or "salvation" is a freely given gift and doxology because the only appropriate response to God's good will is "giving thanks" in the form of prayer and worship.

Because of Jesus Christ and what Calvin understood to be the witness of Scripture, God's good will is at work in all things—in God's free decision to create, in God's continuing activity in the world, and in God's final disposition of all things. It is the central motif in Calvin's description of God's activity of creation (bringing all that is into being out of nothing, *ex nihilo*) and in God's continuing activity within creation (God's sustaining and governing of all events or what Calvin describes as God's "providence").

Many of Calvin's readers have mistakenly concluded that his God is an arbitrary tyrant who rules the world sternly, coldly, and capriciously—a God of sovereign will but not a God of sovereign love. Such a reading of Calvin, although not uncommon, is inaccurate. God's good will is revealed in God's freely given promise in Jesus Christ. Just as the work of God the creator should not be separated from that of God the redeemer, Calvin is seriously misinterpreted if God's good will is not understood in terms of God's love. This is vitally important because if there is a central theme or defining motif in Calvin's theology it is often understood to be the "sovereignty of God." Christian faith, he writes, begins with God's good will, rests in it, and ends in it, but some readers have interpreted him as affirming not God's *good* will but God's *sovereign* will, neglecting the critical point that God's sovereignty is an expression of God's goodness and love. When read in this manner—that God's sovereign will is harsh and capricious—Calvin's interpretation of God's providence becomes fatalism and God's election becomes divine determinism. While Calvin insists that providence and election are both good news about the sovereignty of God's grace and provide consolation and encouragement for Christian faith and life, if the reader forgets that God's will is indeed good and is founded upon "for God so loved the world" (John 3:16), then providence and election become not good news but bad. In his commentary on John 3:16 Calvin writes, "Christ shows us the first cause and as it were source of our salvation. And this He does that no doubt may be left. For there is no calm haven where our minds can rest until we come to God's free love."[11]

Creation as God's Glorious Theater

Before turning to Calvin's interpretation of providence (and in chapter 6 to his discussion of election) it is worth noting what he says about creation. He often describes creation as a "dazzling," "most glorious," or "most beautiful" theater in which God's glory "shines forth," but the consequences of sin are that "scarcely one man in a hundred is a true spectator of it!"[12] God did not create Adam, Calvin argues, until a hospitable world first had been made ready to sustain him. The sun and the stars, the creatures in earth, water, and air, fruits and foods all were created for the human who is the noblest of all God's works.[13] God has "created all things for man's sake."[14]

His description of creation reflects his historical location in the sixteenth century. Calvin's world differs drastically from that of many twenty-first-century readers. Of the twenty-four pages on creation in Book I of the *Institutes*, only the first three examine the natural world (which Calvin believes to be less than six thousand years old), and in the remainder of the chapter, some twenty pages, he discusses angels and demons. Angels are God's creatures—ministers ordained to carry out God's commands, "dispensers and administrators of God's beneficence toward us."[15] The devil is an angel who was created by God and as such is not evil. His evil comes from his perversion and from his revolt and fall. The devil "is God's adversary and ours," an enemy who relentlessly threatens us and who possesses "every conceivable weapon . . . in the science of warfare."[16]

Calvin lived in a world (as Luther put it in "A Mighty Fortress") "with devils filled, who threaten to undo us." For him devils are not simply symbols in the human unconscious or signs of mental disorder; they are not, Calvin insists, simply "evil emotions or perturbations which come upon us from our flesh."[17] The devil is God's enemy, and it is the devil and not God who is the father of lies. Calvin's world may seem bizarre to many of us, although one might make the case that Calvin's understanding of the world is closer to that described in the Bible, in which angels and demons play significant roles, than it is to the Enlightenment-shaped world of many readers today.

Finally, Calvin briefly discusses what we should learn from contemplating creation: first, "to recognize God's powers in the creation of the universe," and, second, to recognize that God has created all things for the good and salvation of human beings and, consequently, "to trust, invoke, praise, and love him."[18]

Not surprisingly Calvin's interpretation of human beings differs significantly from that of most social science departments in universities today. Calvin knows nothing of modern psychology, Freud, the unconscious, or of cultural anthropology, thick description, and philosophical concepts such as intersubjectivity. For Calvin humans are the noblest of all God's created works, the only creatures made in God's image, but like everything else, including creation itself, they are not derived from God's essence, but are created out of nothing. Human beings consist of a body and a soul ("an immortal yet created essence"[19]) that is the nobler of the two. Calvin follows Plato and argues that the image of God in human beings is found in the soul. Soul and body are not only distinct realities but also separate aspects of human being, and Calvin repeatedly describes the soul as a captive in "the prison house of the body." The soul has two "faculties"—the understanding or mind, by means of which reason distinguishes between good and evil, and the will, which is free to choose what the understanding knows to be good and reject that which is evil.[20] The understanding, therefore, is "the leader and governor of the soul," and the will follows the judgments made by the understanding and awaits its bidding. As originally created the will was unencumbered. That is, Adam had "free will," and "prior" to the captivity inflicted on humanity by Adam's sin, human beings had the power to attain eternal life. Free will was "lost," however, in Adam's "fall." Consequently, Adam fell and lost the capacity to will that which his understanding knows to be good, "solely by his own will."[21]

Providence

It is important to pay attention to Calvin's description of creation as populated by angels and demons and to his understanding of human beings as made up of an immortal soul imprisoned in a physical body in order to understand his interpretation of providence that concludes his discussion of God the creator. Providence describes God's "ceaseless activity" by which God not only sustains and preserves the world but also nourishes, cares for, and governs it as well. God's care for creation is not restricted to the "noblest part," that is to human beings, but extends "even to the least sparrow" (a reference to Matthew 10:29, a text Calvin invokes frequently).[22] In the world Calvin finds in the Bible nothing happens by fortune or chance, for "all events are governed by God's secret plan."[23] This does not mean that Calvin denies the reality of contingency. In his commentary on Matthew 10:29 he writes, "In the nature of things itself, I agree there is contingency, but I will say that nothing occurs by the blind turn of fortune where God's will holds the cords."[24] Furthermore, while God is the primary cause in all things, Calvin acknowledges the reality of secondary or intermediary causes, such as nature, the devil, and human agency. His distinction between God's will and human will is the basis for his distinction between primary and secondary causes. Although he claims all things unfold according to God's secret plan and God is "the first cause" of all events, he does not deny the reality of "secondary" or intermediary causes. God's providence is the determining principle in all things, but God's will works sometimes "through an intermediary, sometimes without an intermediary, sometimes contrary to every intermediary."[25] While these distinctions may still seem too simplistic to a modern reader, Calvin does recognize something of the complexity of sorting out human agency, natural causes, and divine agency. Although Calvin's understanding of the cosmos bears little resemblance to Stephen Hawking's, his interpretation of providence is not a scientific account of reality but a theological one, derived from Scripture not physics. One does not need to know about black holes in order to affirm that Christians should trust God in all things.

God does not idly observe from heaven what takes place in the world; rather, God governs all events. This understanding of providence is simply an extension of Calvin's understanding of the sovereignty of God's will. For him both the Bible and human experience demonstrate that God so "regulates all things that nothing takes place without his deliberation."[26] If we think about God this way we can perhaps better understand how Calvin must have heard Farel's words that fateful (to use a term Calvin might not appreciate) night in 1536 when Farel told him that it was God's will that he stay, give up his plans for a scholarly life in Basel, and assist the cause of reform in Geneva.

Calvin distinguishes between general and special providence. The first affirms that God "directs everything by his incomprehensible wisdom and disposes it to his own end."[27] The second, special or particular providence, claims that God not only watches over and directs creation, but that God "so attends to the regulation of individual events" that everything takes place according to God's "set plan." Nothing occurs by fate or by chance. All events are to be understood finally and ultimately in relation to God's sovereign good will. Calvin does not deny general providence—that God watches over humanity and "sheds upon heaven and earth an ordinary power, by which they are supplied with food"—but he insists the Bible claims more than this. God not only provides food for the world in general, but both the fruitfulness of one year and the famine of another are God's specific blessing and curse.[28] In Question 279 of his *Geneva Catechism* Calvin raises the question of why the rich, who have an abundance of good things, should petition God to give them "this day" their bread. What matters, he responds, is not how much one possesses, because possessions will not be fruitful and efficacious unless God enables them to be such. Even if we possess all things (indeed, especially if we do so), "we have nothing, except we receive them hour by hour from the hand of God, as is necessary and sufficient for us."[29]

An obvious problem arises with Calvin's claim that all events—not just some events, but all events—are ruled or governed by God's good will. Does that not make God responsible for sin and evil? How can God condemn human sin if it is in some sense what God wills? Does God have two wills—what God wills for the world in the commandments of the covenant and what God wills in regard to sin and evil? Calvin vigorously rejects the distinction some theologians make between God's permitting will and God's governing will. Righteousness is not what God wills and sin and evil what God permits. Is God then the author of sin and evil? Not so, Calvin insists. He resolves the conundrum not by philosophical argument but by turning to biblical narratives, for example Luke's description of the passion and crucifixion of Christ. On the one hand, Luke tells his readers that Jesus is executed by the Jewish leaders of the Temple and by Herod and Pilate, who are responsible for his death. On the other hand, Luke writes that Jesus' death was what God planned and decreed (Acts 4:28). Is God the Father then responsible for the crucifixion of the Son? Is God the father guilty of "child abuse," as some theologians today allege? Calvin sees no conflict here. God's will is not at war with itself, "nor does it change, nor does it pretend not to will what he wills."[30] God's will is unified and simple. The problem is not with God but with human "mental incapacity." God's will appears "manifold" and even contradictory, but, quoting Augustine, Calvin argues that there is "a great difference between what is fitting for man to will and what is fitting for God." God can accomplish the goodness that God wills "even through the bad wills of evil men."[31] Judas may sin by betraying his Lord, but God's will that the world be redeemed by the death of the Son does not make Judas less culpable or God less glorious. God "knows right well," Calvin insists, "how to use evil instruments to do good."[32]

For Calvin God's providence is unequivocally good news. It does not relieve Christians of individual responsibility for what happens to them, nor does it excuse them from exercising common sense, but confidence in God's good will enables them to trust that "all things happen by God's plan," that God will not suffer anything to happen that will not finally result in their ultimate good and salvation. Providence, therefore, is a deeply pastoral doctrine. Properly understood it should lead the Christian to "Gratitude of mind for the favorable outcome of things, patience in adversity, and also incredible freedom from worry about the future."[33] The answer to Question 26 of the Heidelberg Catechism of 1563 (written the year before Calvin's death) reflects Calvin's emphasis on the governance of God's good will in all things. The question asks what it means to believe (in the words of The Apostles' Creed) in "God the Father Almighty, Maker of Heaven and Earth?" The catechism answers:

I trust in him so completely that I have no doubt he will provide me with all things necessary for body and soul. Moreover, whatever evil he sends upon me in this troubled life he will turn to my good, for he is able to do it, being Almighty God, and he is determined to do it, being a faithful Father.[34]

Although Heidelberg's confidence in God's omnipotence, God's good will in all things, is an impressive statement of classical Christian faith, it probably sounds strange, perhaps even morally offensive, to many contemporary readers. It sounds strange because, although it distinguishes between primary and secondary causes, between divine and human agency, it still reflects a world filled with angels, demons, and witchcraft, a world in which God is the primary factor in all events. Although Calvin was a Renaissance humanist and a contemporary of Copernicus (1473–1543), the scientific discoveries of Galileo (born in 1564, the same year Calvin died) and Isaac Newton (1642–1727), not to mention the theories of Stephen Hawking, were unknown to him. His universe was still one in which God's supernatural intervention in the natural order, described in Scripture, was not a hermeneutical problem.

Although widespread epidemics and plagues and the butchery of war were no less a reality in the sixteenth century than they are in the twentieth and the twenty-first, it has become difficult, if not impossible, for many modern Christians to see a direct, causal relation between God and events such as the Holocaust or the global scourge of AIDS. Although Calvin could affirm that what Christians know in Jesus Christ is God's sovereign good will, many contemporary Christians are unable to find God's good will in all things. If they use the language of God's sovereignty at all, they are more likely to speak of God's sovereign love than of God's sovereign will, and this shift represents more than a change in academic theological discourse. It points to a "sea change" of sorts in contemporary Christian experience and piety.

Calvin's understanding of God's providence is inseparable from his conviction that what God wills is good and that all things, even those that seem irredeemable, are finally made to serve God's purposes. Calvin was able to make those affirmations because he had no doubt about the ultimate destiny of all things within the purposes of God. Many contemporary Christians do not share that conviction that all of history finally serves what God wills. While Calvin's world and his understanding of God may seem too strange and too simple to some Christians today, one can imagine the many questions Calvin might have about a Christian faith that has made its peace with evil by placing it outside of God's transforming and redeeming reach.[35]

Questions

1. Calvin follows Plato in distinguishing between a human being's soul and body. It is the former that is the "image of God" and as such is nobler than the body. Is this the same understanding of human beings that one finds in the Bible? What are the consequences of understanding the human body as "the prison house of the soul"?

2. Calvin understands God's providence to entail the claim that God governs all things. What does Calvin mean by that? Do you agree with him?

3. God's sovereign good will is at the heart of Calvin's understanding of God. Many contemporary Christians prefer to speak of God's love rather than God's will. Why do they do that? Is that a significant change in how people understand God?

THE MEDIATOR AS PROPHET, PRIEST, AND KING

I n his discussion of God the creator in Book I of the *Institutes*, Calvin describes human beings as uniquely created in God's image. In Book II he turns to the knowledge of God the redeemer, the incarnation of the Word in Jesus Christ, and once again describes human beings, not just as God's good creation, which they continue to be, but as creatures deformed by sin who are forgiven and restored to life before God by the mediator, Jesus Christ.

Sin and the Second Adam

Human beings cannot be understood properly by looking first at Adam in the opening chapters of Genesis, because Adam represents not only created humanity but its distortion and loss of original righteousness as well. God's image in Adam was "not totally annihilated and destroyed," but was "so vitiated and almost blotted out that nothing remains after the ruin except what is confused, mutilated, and disease-ridden."[1] It is in Christ that humanity recovers what was lost in Adam; "the beginning of our recovery of salvation is in that restoration which we obtain through Christ, who also is called the Second Adam for the reason that he restores us to true and complete integrity."[2] It is Christ, not Adam, who enables sinful people to know what they were created to be, what it is they no longer are, and what they shall become when they are finally, fully regenerated in Christ.

It is significant that Calvin discusses sin at the beginning of his interpretation of God the redeemer. The theological point is that sin can be known only from the perspective of God's grace in Jesus Christ the redeemer. Why? Because the consequence of sin is that "blind self-love is innate in all mortals."[3] Human nature, corrupted by sin, "seeks nothing more eagerly than to be flattered," and it is this flattery that opens the door to self-deception; "it so deceives as to drive those who assent to it into utter ruin."[4] The problem is not just in the intellect, but in the heart and the will as well. Original righteousness, the ability not to sin (*posse non peccare*) has been lost in Adam and now the truth about human beings is that they are not able not to sin (*non posse non peccare*). Humanity's only hope is for a redeemer who will release it from its captivity to its own self-deception.

What is this sin that has the power of self-deception and just how pervasive is it? Are all people sinners? Is every human act tainted by sin? Calvin's answer to these questions reflects the pervasive influence of Augustine and Luther. From the perspective of God's redemption in Jesus Christ, Calvin turns to the "first sin" in Genesis 3 in order to understand the nature of sin. In Book II of the *Institutes* and in his commentary on

Genesis (1554) he interprets the "first sin" not as Adam's and Eve's "gluttonous intemperance" in regard to the fruit of the forbidden tree, which he considers a childish interpretation of Adam's "defection." Augustine's claim that pride was the beginning of all evil is closer to the truth, but even that is "too narrow" an interpretation of the first sin. Sin for Calvin is unfaithfulness or unbelief. "Unfaithfulness, then, was the root of the Fall" and from it arose ambition, pride, and ungratefulness.[5] If God's good will is to be found in life lived according to God's commandments, it is not surprising that sin is unfaithfulness or life lived in disobedience to the good that God wills.

And how does the sin of Adam and Eve affect the rest of humanity? Calvin describes original sin as "a hereditary depravity and corruption of our nature, diffused into all parts of the soul," but the pervasiveness of sin is to be understood theologically and not biologically.[6] Adam represents all of humanity and all people receive from God the consequences of Adam's sin. In his commentary on John 3:6, Calvin argues that the universality of sin is not the result of human reproduction. Sin is universal because all humanity is "in Adam." Just as all people have an original righteousness in Adam, so too it is lost in Adam because "the corruption of all mankind in the person of Adam alone did not proceed from generation, but from the ordinance of God."[7] Or as he puts it in the *Institutes*, we should understand the contagion of sin "not as if we, guiltless and undeserving, bore the guilt of his [Adam's] offense but in the sense that, since we through his transgression have become entangled in the curse, he is said to make us guilty."[8] Every human being then is implicated in Adam's sin, and "original" sin refers not only to the "first" sin but also to its universal implications. All have sinned in Adam, and they sin not because they are forced to but of "necessity," because the will is "enslaved" or in bondage to sin.

Not only have all sinned, but there is no human act, no aspect of human being and existence that is untainted by sin. Humanity's desires are disordered; what (or who) should be loved with all one's heart, soul, and strength is loved too little, and what should be loved properly only in relation to its goodness is loved too much. There is, therefore, no aspect of a person's being that "is immune from sin and all that proceeds from him is to be imputed to sin."[9]

Both the understanding and the will have been disabled by sin. Echoing Paul in Romans 7:14-20 ("For I do not do the good I want, but the evil I do not want is what I do"), Calvin concludes that although those who have received God's grace in Jesus Christ may desire to follow what is good they cannot do so "except by the impulsion of the Holy Spirit." The consequence of "the Fall" is a universality of sin most apparent in the activity of the human will. Sin is a paradox. Human beings sin "freely," but also of necessity. They freely and voluntarily choose to sin and at the same time they cannot choose not to sin; that is, they sin necessarily. Like Augustine and Luther before him, Calvin is drawn to Romans 3:23 ff. ("all have sinned and fall short of the glory of God"). If anyone does a good work it is not an indication that a remnant of righteousness persists in the soul and somehow survived the ravages of sin, but evidence of God at work, even in the midst of devastation and death, bringing good out of evil, for "everything good in the will is the work of grace alone."[10] Everything good that humanity does, without exception, is by grace alone. Calvin vigorously rejects any suggestion that sinful human beings can somehow "cooperate" with God's free gift of grace and good will. Those who believe that human beings have within themselves "the power to work in partnership with God's grace . . . are most wretchedly deluding themselves."[11] Such delusions or self-deceptions are the power of sin, a power to which everyone is enslaved.

Because the whole human race perished in the person of Adam, there is no escape from the captivity of sin and the death that follows. Both Calvin and the writers of the Heidelberg Catechism of 1563 echo the conclusion that Paul draws concerning the consequences of sin: "Wretched man that I am! Who will rescue me from this body of death?" (Rom. 7:24). Sinners have no hope if they look within themselves; rather, "the hope of all the godly has ever reposed in Christ *alone*."[12] Sinners live by grace alone because it is by Christ alone that they are rescued from the wretchedness of their "body of death." Like Luther and Melanchthon, Calvin recognized that the gospel is not just one good Word among many, but that Word alone which is good news. At the heart of the Protestant Reformation are words like "only" and "alone." The Scots Confession of 1560 begins in its first sentence with a litany of "alones." "We confess and acknowledge one God *alone*, to whom *alone* we must cleave, whom *alone* we must serve, whom *only* we must worship, and in whom *alone* we put our trust" (emphasis added).

Calvin's interpretation of sin follows a Christian "logic" similar to that of Augustine, Luther, Zwingli, Melanchthon, Bucer, and many others. Sin describes the human condition; it pervades every thought, word, and act. It is a principality and power, an intruder, in God's good creation. Because of sin's capacity to deceive, humanity's enslavement is not apparent except from the perspective of redemption, and redemption is a reality only in the person of the mediator, Jesus Christ.

The Mediator

The key to this Christian "logic" is the mediator. Sin cannot be understood apart from God's grace in Jesus Christ; nor is Christian faith and life, as a response of gratitude, intelligible apart from the person of the mediator. It is in this sense that Calvin's theology is "Christocentric." For him the good news of Christian faith is that God wills the world good, and the basis or foundation for that affirmation is "the truth of the freely given promise in Christ."[13]

Just as Calvin had no interest in revising (or reforming) the Church's understanding of the Trinity, so too he unequivocally affirmed the Christology of the Council of Chalcedon (451). In order to redeem sins, the mediator had to be both truly God and truly human—truly God because only God can forgive sins and truly human in order that all who have sinned in Adam might be saved in Christ. Because human beings are in bondage to sin, they cannot redeem themselves and can only hope for someone who will do for them what they cannot do for themselves. The mediator, in the language of Chalcedon, is one person in two natures—fully God and fully human. As Calvin put it, "The situation would surely have been hopeless had the very majesty of God not descended to us, since it was not in our power to ascend to him."[14] Even if Adam had not sinned, the human condition "would have been too lowly" for humanity to stand before God without a mediator.[15] To be the mediator, "it was necessary for the Son of God to become for us 'Immanuel, that is, God with us' [Isa. 7:14; Matt. 1:23] and in such a way that his divinity and our human nature might by mutual connection grow together."[16] At the same time it is no less necessary that the mediator be fully human. Christ could not restore sinners to God's grace without taking "what was ours as to impute what was his to us, and to make what was his by nature ours by grace."[17]

Given the centrality of Jesus Christ in Calvin's understanding of the gospel, the brevity of his discussion in the *Institutes* of the "person" of Christ (some thirty pages) is perhaps surprising. Particularly significant is Calvin's use of the term "mediator" to describe the person of Christ. Calvin has no interest in extended theological speculation about the mystery of the incarnation. Would the Word have become flesh—still have "fashioned for himself a body from our body, flesh from our flesh, bone from our bones, that he might become one with us"[18]—if Adam had not sinned? Rather than becoming human, might the Son of God have "taken upon himself the nature of an ass?"[19] Questions such as these, Calvin argues, are "foolish curiosity."[20] Not only are they foolish ("vague speculations that captivate the frivolous and the seekers after novelty"[21]), they miss the point of the incarnation—namely that the incarnation has no other purpose than the redemption of sinful humanity.

Calvin uses the term "mediator" to describe the Word incarnate because there must be no separation between who Jesus is as the Word incarnate and what he does. While there is a theological distinction between what is sometimes referred to as the "person" of Christ and the "work" of Christ, they must not be separated, and the term "mediator" points to the inseparability of the two. Mediator is who Jesus is, and mediation between God and sinners is what Jesus does. The incarnation is not "logical" in the sense that human reason can fully fathom it, but a mystery rooted in God's good will, in God's "heavenly decree." "We well know why Christ was promised from the beginning: to restore the fallen world and to succor lost men."[22] Calvin finds the origin and "reason" for the incarnation in the mystery of God's electing will that creation be redeemed.

Prophet, Priest, and King

Calvin's interpretation of the Old Testament means Christians cannot understand who Jesus is as the Christ, as the Mediator, apart from the history of Israel. In the *Geneva Catechism* of 1545 the minister asks the child what is the meaning of the title "Christ" in reference to Jesus of Nazareth. The child answers: "it signifies that he is appointed by his Father to be King, Priest, and Prophet." Asked how one can know this, the child replies because Scripture "applies authority to these three uses, attributes these three offices to Christ."[23] Similarly, in the *Institutes*, Calvin gives an entire chapter (II, 15) to an explanation of Jesus' threefold office (*munus triplex*) as prophet, priest, and king.

He interprets Christ's prophetic office as that of a teacher of doctrine. Jesus' teaching provides the sum of all doctrine and in his teaching "all parts of perfect wisdom are contained."[24] Like the rest of Israel's prophets Jesus is a herald and a witness to the Father's grace, but Jesus is also unique among Israel's prophets. The doctrine he teaches is perfect and outside him there is nothing worth knowing. Calvin's interpretation of Jesus' prophetic office ignores the gospels' description of Jesus as an exorcist, healer, and performer of miracles. In *A Harmony of the Gospels*, published in 1555, as in the *Institutes*, Jesus is not so much an exorcist and healer as he is a teacher of perfect doctrine. Nor does Calvin seem to be sensitive to what many Christians today have learned from liberation theologians about God's preferential option for the poor in the person and ministry of Jesus.

The 1559 edition of the *Institutes* gives twice as many pages to Jesus' office as king as it does to the prophetic office. Jesus' "royal" office is not earthly but spiritual, and it promises both the everlasting preservation of the church and the hope of immortality. This relative neglect of Jesus' prophetic office is reflected in the *Geneva Catechism* of 1545. In response to the child's question as to why the Apostles' Creed passes directly from Jesus' birth to his death ("born of the virgin Mary, suffered under Pontius Pilate"), the minister answers, "Because nothing is dealt with here, except what so pertains to our redemption." That text is often quoted by modern theologians who find classical Christology inadequate because of its reduction of incarnation to the formula of one person, two natures. Jesus' identity, like that of every human being, is inextricably linked to what he says and does and to the pivotal events in his life. For many twentieth-century theologians, the stories of Jesus' life and ministry in the Gospels should not be limited simply to what he said, to texts such as his Sermon on the Mount and his parables about the kingdom of God. Jesus also casts out demons, heals disease, brings people back to life, and tells his disciples to both proclaim God's kingdom and to heal and cast out demons. Contrary to the *Geneva Catechism*, the story of Jesus' life has everything to do with who he is and what the New Testament means when it calls Jesus the Christ and the mediator.

In his exposition of Jesus' threefold office, Calvin devotes most of his attention to Jesus' priestly office. Given his use of the term mediator to describe Jesus it is perhaps not surprising that Calvin emphasizes Jesus as priest, nor that he is especially drawn to the Letter to the Hebrews and its interpretation of Jesus as the high priest who atones for sin and reconciles humanity to God. Because Christ alone is without sin, he is able to obtain God's forgiveness of sinners by giving himself as a sacrifice to God's righteous judgment. Referring to Hebrews 9:22, Calvin describes Christ as priest "because by the sacrifice of his death he blotted out our own guilt and made satisfaction for our sins."[25] Just as he used Israel's prophets to interpret the ministry of Jesus and then argued that Jesus is unique among them, so he does the same with Jesus' priestly office. Like Israel's priests, Jesus offers sacrifice to God for human sin, but Jesus is also unique among Israel's priests in that he not only offers sacrifice but is himself the one sacrifice capable of redeeming sinful humanity; "in Christ there was a new and different order, in which the same one was to be both priest and sacrifice."[26] Christ's death, as Calvin interprets it, is a form of what is sometimes described as the satisfaction theory of the atonement; "to make satisfaction for our redemption a form of death had to be chosen in which he might free us both by transferring our condemnation to himself and by taking our guilt upon himself."[27] Christ satisfies God's righteous judgment on human sin by taking the place of all humanity; he "came forth as true man and took the person and the name of Adam in order to take Adam's place in obeying the Father, to present our flesh as the price of satisfaction to God's righteous judgment, and, in the same flesh, to pay the penalty that we had deserved."[28]

Modern theologians have raised numerous objections to the various forms of satisfaction and substitution theories of the atonement, not the least of which is that they seem to place God in opposition to God's self by pitting God's righteousness and wrath against God's grace and love, or by suggesting that God the Father is righteous and just while the Son of God is loving and merciful. Admittedly, Calvin does argue that apart from Christ sinful human beings know God only as hostile to them "and his hand is armed for our destruction," and that God has "been our enemy until he was reconciled to us through Christ."[29] But he also recognizes "some sort of contradiction arises here" and resolves the difficulty, as he does many others, by appealing to God's accommodation to humanity's finitude and limited capacity to understand. The Bible describes God this way, he argues, in order that human beings might comprehend both the full despair of sin and the wonder of Christ's grace. There is no division within the Trinity between the Father's righteousness and the Son's love. Whatever else one may say about Calvin it would be difficult to accuse him of a superficial knowledge of the Bible. He too knew John 3:16, and he insisted that the Father gave his Son for one reason only—in order that a sinful world might not perish—and because "he is moved by pure and freely given love of us to receive us into grace."[30]

Although the mediator, who is prophet, priest, and king, is one person in two natures, Calvin also insists that the two natures be distinguished from one another in order that they not be confused and that there be no suggestion that humanity has been deified. He agrees with Chalcedon's insistence that the two natures not become confused and indistinguishable. Christ's divinity is "so joined and united with his humanity that each retains its distinctive nature unimpaired, and yet these two natures constitute one Christ."[31] The Bible affirms a "communion" of the two natures but some qualities are proper only to his divinity while others are proper only to his humanity. Not surprisingly he finds John's Gospel to be the clearest statement of Christ's identity. When Christ says, "Before Abraham was, I am" (John 8:58), Calvin insists Christ is "claiming for himself what is proper for his divinity." And when we read in Luke 2:52 that Christ "increased in wisdom and in years, and in divine and human favor," Calvin concludes this refers "solely to Christ's humanity." Christ is not at one time God and at another time human, because we read "neither of deity nor of humanity alone, but of both at once," and it is because Christ is both at once that he has "from the Father the power of remitting sins [John 1:29], of raising to life whom he will, of bestowing righteousness, holiness, salvation."[32] In short, because Christ is neither simply God nor simply human but both at once, he is the mediator.

Calvin's concern to distinguish between Christ's two natures leads him to "something marvelous" and what has come to be known as the "extra Calvinisticum"—namely, that while the Son of God descended from heaven and, in the language of the Apostles' Creed, was "born of the virgin Mary, suffered under Pontius Pilate, was crucified, dead, and buried," he did so in such a way that "he was not confined therein . . . the Son of God descended from heaven in such a way that, without leaving heaven . . . he continuously filled the world even as he had done from the beginning!"[33] Christ's deity, therefore, is ubiquitous, but his human body is not. As Wilhelm Niesel put it, this does not mean that God is both revealed in Jesus Christ and elsewhere as well. God discloses God's self only in Jesus Christ, but this does not mean that Christ is different from other human beings only in degree. "In Jesus Christ we are faced not merely by enhanced nature, but the fact is that there God Himself stands revealed to us."[34]

Calvin's distinction between Christ's two natures and what is appropriate to say of one but not the other had significant consequences for his interpretation of the Lord's Supper (as we shall see in chapter 7). This is an important example of his "christo-centricity"; how his understanding of the person of Christ and the distinction between the two natures bears decisively on his understanding of the presence of Christ in the Lord's Supper and the sense in which the church is and is not the body of Christ.

The distinction between the two natures led Calvin to conclude that texts such as 1 Corinthians 2:8 (that the Lord of glory was crucified) could not mean that God suffers and dies. "Surely God does not have blood, does not suffer, cannot be touched with hands."[35] These are things that refer to Christ's human nature and are "transferred improperly, although not without reason, to his divinity." However, Calvin's claim that God cannot suffer has been rejected by many contemporary theologians, including Jürgen Moltmann, who argues that texts such as 1 Corinthians 1:18-25 suggest that God's power is precisely the weakness of the cross, the power of suffering love, that the use of the "apathy axiom" (that God cannot suffer) reflects a Hellenistic understanding of deity rather than a biblical understanding of God's pathos, and that interpretations like Calvin's fail to understand Christ's death as an event in the life of the triune life (that is, that the Father truly suffers the loss of the Son). Calvin, no doubt, would wonder whether Moltmann has not made the suffering love of the triune God captive to his own ideological and political agenda.[36]

Questions

1. If sin can be known only from the perspective of God's redeeming grace in Jesus Christ, why does Calvin discuss sin in the *Institutes* before he turns to Christ the Mediator?

2. In the *Geneva Catechism* Calvin says that nothing of significance for salvation is to be found in Christ's ministry. Why does he say that? Do you agree with him?

3. Calvin argues that Christ's humanity should not be confused with his deity, and that God, therefore, cannot suffer. Do you agree with him?

CHAPTER SIX

THE EFFICACIOUS SPIRIT

A quick, first glance at the *Institutes* might suggest that Calvin had little or no interest in the Holy Spirit. Such an impression would certainly fit with a common perception of him (and the theological tradition of "Calvinism") as "God's frozen chosen," an intellectual form of Christian faith that knows nothing of the spontaneity and vitality of the Spirit and, like the Lion in *The Wizard of Oz*, desperately needs a heart. Calvin's theology, with its emphasis on the knowledge of God, might seem like it is more suitable for the academy and the classroom than for the church and the sanctuary. Such a conclusion, however, would be a serious misinterpretation. A closer reading suggests just the opposite. As we have seen, for Calvin what faith "knows" is just as much a matter of the heart as of the intellect. It is a knowledge that is inseparably related to "piety." To know God is to revere and love God because one has experienced Christ's "benefits." Revering and loving are just as much, if not more so, activities of the heart as of the mind. But what are these "benefits" Calvin refers to, and how does one come to experience and "know" them with both the heart and the mind? In the third and fourth books of the *Institutes* Calvin answers these questions.

The Spirit's Gift of the Benefits of Christ

As Calvin's definition of faith suggests, Christ's benefits include the knowledge of God's benevolence—God's "good will"—founded upon the truth of the freely given promise in Christ. All this is the work of the Holy Spirit, who, for Calvin, does one thing above all else. The Spirit binds, unites, "engrafts" (Paul's metaphor) people to Jesus Christ. They do not choose Christ or the faith that is "founded" on him; rather he chooses them and by means of his Spirit gives them the gift of faith. The Spirit enables them to find new life in Christ and to experience Christ living within them. When this happens, Christ no longer remains "outside of us"—merely an interesting historical figure, whose life and suffering remain "useless and of no value for us."[1] When the Spirit binds people to Christ, God's freely given promise of mercy and forgiveness becomes theirs; "we make them ours by inwardly embracing them," and in so doing discover peace—"an assurance that renders the conscience calm and peaceful before God's judgment."[2]

In the middle of the twentieth century the American Reformed theologian H. Richard Niebuhr described revelation as a transition from knowing Jesus as a figure of "external history"—an important person in world history—to knowing him as a figure in one's "internal history." Jesus Christ is "this intelligible event which makes all other events intelligible."[3] Niebuhr did not attribute this development to the Holy Spirit as clearly as Calvin does, nor did his understanding of internal history have Calvin's vibrant, almost mystical, sense of being in Christ.

Calvin's discussion of the Holy Spirit at the beginning of Book III of the *Institutes* consists of only six brief pages. It would be a serious mistake, however, to conclude that this is all that Calvin has to say about the Spirit and that the brevity of this chapter is evidence the Spirit is unimportant to him. This is not the first time he has mentioned the Spirit. His description of the knowledge of God and the role of the Bible is unintelligible apart from the Spirit. It has been a persistent theme throughout the first two books of the *Institutes*, and a strong case could be made that not just the first chapter of the third book but the entirety of the third and fourth books, comprising nearly one thousand pages (or two-thirds of the *Institutes*), is a discussion of the person and work of the Holy Spirit. That may be why Benjamin B. Warfield, a theologian at Princeton Theological Seminary in the late nineteenth and early twentieth centuries, described Calvin as above all else "a theologian of the Holy Spirit."[4]

The Spirit is "the bond by which Christ effectually unites us to himself."[5] Apart from the Spirit "no one can taste either the fatherly favor of God or the beneficence of Christ."[6] To use Niebuhr's categories, it is the Spirit who enables Christ to become more than an interesting historical figure, to become a transforming presence in a person's "internal history," and that transformation is what Calvin means by "Christ's benefits" and what others have referred to as "the Christian life."

A Portrait of Christian Life

The third book of the *Institutes* is Calvin's description of what the Spirit does in binding Christians to Christ. It can be read in several ways. It can be read as a list of theological themes or doctrines that describe the Christian life: faith (chapter 2); regeneration (chapters 3–5); sanctification (chapters 6–10); justification (chapters 11–18); Christian freedom (chapter 19); prayer (chapter 20); election or predestination (chapters 21–24); and resurrection (chapter 25). Or it can be read not as a list of theological topics, but, given Calvin's frequent use of the metaphors of journey, pilgrimage, and path, as a description of the "stages" in the Christian journey toward redemption. Yet another way to read this material is not as a list of doctrines or a series of steps down a path, but as a portrait or landscape of the Christian life. The metaphors of portrait and landscape may be more appealing than those of a list of doctrines or a series of stages because there is no causal or sequential order to Calvin's description of the Christian life. The Christian does not first experience regeneration and then move on or "graduate" to the subsequent stages of sanctification and justification. Book III, together with Book IV, is Calvin's description of the landscape of the Christian life, what is sometimes referred to as "the order of salvation" (the *ordo salutis*). This "order," however, is not a list or a sequence, but the full panorama of a landscape. It is a portrait, a description of what the Spirit's transforming grace in Jesus Christ looks like, an effort to see the Christian life in its coherence and its wholeness.

In binding or uniting sinners to Christ, the Spirit gives them the gift of faith, which Calvin describes as "the principal work of the Holy Spirit."[7] Because it is a gift, faith is not in the most important sense a human act. Ingenuity, creativity, and the imagination are, of course, involved whenever humans express faith, but the primary agent in faith is the Spirit and the appropriate human response—exercising ingenuity, creativity, and the imagination—is gratitude, doxology, and the service of God in the world.

As Calvin put it, faith is "knowledge of God's will toward us, perceived from his Word,"[8] and it is the Spirit who enables that Word to become "efficacious" in both the heart and the mind. Calvin finds value in Augustine's rationale. Why, when two people hear the same Word—the promise of God's grace in Jesus Christ—does one believe and the other not? It is not that the one is less sinful than the other or more intelligent or more loving than the other. Why is faith given to the one and not to the other? Calvin answers in words taken from Augustine's sermons: "it is of God. . . . This means much to me. It is an abyss, the depth of the cross. I can exclaim in wonder; I cannot demonstrate it through disputation."[9] It is the mystery of God's grace that the Spirit moves the heart and mind of one person but not those of the other.

Sanctification and Justification

The Spirit gives Christians faith that by means of the Mediator, Jesus Christ, God forgives their sin and makes them a new creation, or, as Calvin puts it, "the sum of the gospel is held to consist in repentance and forgiveness of sins."[10] Somewhat surprisingly he chooses to describe the effects of faith in terms of regeneration, repentance, and sanctification before he turns to justification and the forgiveness of sins. The only reason he gives for reversing the more traditional order in which justification precedes sanctification is that if repentance is rightly understood "it will better appear how man is justified by faith alone, and simple pardon."[11] He adds two important comments. First, the distinction between justification and sanctification is theologically artificial because justification and sanctification are a double or twofold grace, a *duplex gratia*. That means, first, that sanctification—the "actual holiness of life" that comes with being bound by the Spirit to Christ—and justification by faith should not be separated from one another. They are two sides of the same coin, dialectically related, and one cannot properly be understood apart from the other. Second, repentance and sanctification not only follow from faith, but are born of it. In other words, Calvin makes clear that by beginning his discussion of the benefits of Christ with repentance and sanctification he is not suggesting that faith is wholly a human act and forgiveness God's gracious response. The benefits of Christ are not a reward for doing the right thing—believing—but an undeserved gift of God's Spirit. God's grace and forgiveness are not God's reward for "good works"; rather it is God's grace and forgiveness that precede human acts of faithfulness and that make human works "good."

Why does Calvin invite this critical misunderstanding of the Christian life—that God's grace is a response to human faith rather than what makes faith possible—by beginning with repentance and sanctification rather than justification? He hints at an answer. He seems concerned that some readers might conclude that the good news of God's forgiveness by faith alone might lead to what twentieth-century theologian Dietrich Bonhoeffer described as "cheap grace"—a gospel without discipleship.[12] "Surely," Calvin writes, "no one can embrace the grace of the gospel without betaking himself from the errors of his past life into the right way, and applying his whole effort to the practice of repentance."[13]

Faith and repentance are inseparable but they are not the same thing. Both are gifts of the one Spirit who binds sinners to Christ in order that they may receive his benefits.

By repentance Calvin means conversion. To repent is to turn, to turn away from sin or unbelief and to turn to God; "it is the true turning of our life to God, a turning that arises from a pure and earnest fear of him; and it consists in the mortification of our flesh and of the old man, and in the vivification of the Spirit."[14] It is more than a simple change of mind. It is a transformation, a dying to one way of life and a rebirth to another, one that is prompted by recognition of sin and a fear of God's righteous judgment. It takes place "through continual and sometimes even slow advances," and is a lifelong process that "will end only at death."[15]

Calvin's description of the Christian life is a religious classic. It was excerpted from the *Institutes* during his lifetime, published separately, translated into English, and became a major influence on first English and then American Puritanism. His concern in this material is to provide his readers with "a pattern for the conduct of life" or a description of how the Christian life is to be rightly ordered. He does not do so by describing Christian virtues, such as faith, hope, and love, which he acknowledges can be found in the sermons of theologians in the early church, but by focusing on Christ, because in him God the Father has "stamped for us the likeness to which he would have us conform."[16]

Calvin's description of the Christian life reflects Matthew 16:24/Mark 8:34: "Then Jesus told his disciples, 'If any want to become my followers, let them deny themselves and take up their cross and follow me.'" The Christian life, therefore, consists of three themes: self-denial, cross-bearing, and meditation on the future life. The sum of the gospel, Calvin argues, is self-denial. There are occasionally passages in the *Institutes* in which Calvin the theologian gives way to Calvin the preacher and the poet. Commenting on 1 Corinthians 6:19, and Paul's claim that "you are not your own," Calvin writes that Jesus' call to those who would be his disciples to deny themselves and follow him means, "We are not our own: let not our reason nor our will, therefore, sway our plans and deeds. . . . Conversely, we are God's: let us therefore live for him and die for him." The first step in the Christian life is to "depart" from oneself in order that one may turn "wholly to the bidding of God's Spirit" and do nothing except to God's glory.[17] Self-denial means both devotion to God and doing good to the neighbor; "whatever man you meet who needs your aid, you have no reason to refuse to help him."[18]

Second, to deny oneself is to take up one's cross. Christian self-denial entails cross-bearing. In *A Harmony of the Gospels* Calvin interprets Matthew 16:24 to be a short rule for imitating Christ that has two aspects: "denial of ourselves and the voluntary bearing of the cross."[19] The latter does not refer simply to the everyday problems everyone experiences, but to the struggles freely and patiently suffered by those whom God has called to discipleship. "This denial is far reaching . . . we are prepared to be reduced to nothing so that God may live and reign in us." The crosses to which God calls Jesus' disciples are indispensable to the Spirit's process of sanctification. The cross teaches hope for the future—not Stoic resignation, but Christian patience and obedience. It teaches Christians to live according to God's good will rather than their own, to be able to pray "Your will be done, on earth as it is in heaven" (Matt. 6:10).

Finally, self-denial and cross-bearing teach the Christian to turn away from and have contempt for what Calvin calls "the vanity of this life" and to "meditate upon the future life," the eternal life Christians have in Christ's resurrection. This longing for eternal life and contempt for the world does not mean ingratitude for this life. This earthly life, Calvin insists, is a gift from God that should be received with gratitude and counted "among the gifts of divine generosity which are not at all to be rejected."[20] The Christian journey or pilgrimage, however, does not conclude with this life.

Many Christians today may find Calvin's description of the Christian life odd, and perhaps even repugnant. It may sound masochistic, an "otherworldly" denial of this life, a passive acceptance of political structures and social and economic systems that are unjust in anticipation of a heavenly kingdom free of these evils. For women living in patriarchal societies, people of color in racist communities, and those who have been the victims of Western colonialism sin may not be an inflated sense of self that takes the form of pride as much as it is an undeveloped and diminished sense of self-identity. For those whose primary sin is not thinking too much of themselves but too little, who choose not to live before God but to flee and to hide in the shadows, a description of the Christian life as self-denial, cross-bearing (patience in the midst of adversity), and meditation on the future life may seem to reflect the uncritical perspective of a theologian unaware of sexism, racism, and classism. There is surely something right about this indictment of Calvin. Indeed, Calvin's own theology compels us to acknowledge that he was himself, like every other theologian, blind to the sinfulness of many of his political, economic, social, and cultural assumptions, just as are those who bring the indictment against him. To be in sin, Calvin understood, is to be self-deceived, and it is the Spirit alone who enables sinful minds to overcome the myopia of sin and to see, if only partially and incompletely, the truth about themselves and their world.

Did Calvin write from a position of privilege? As we saw in chapter 1, a common misunderstanding of him is that he ruled both the church and the city of Geneva with unchallenged authority. It is important to remember, however, that he was a French refugee in Geneva, a city in which the growing presence of other religious refugees was a serious political, economic, and social issue. He was driven out of Geneva in 1538 and his political opponents were only finally defeated nine years before he died. He lived in Geneva for over twenty years before he was offered a form of citizenship, and was never a wealthy man. The categories of "insider" and "outsider" are inadequate to describe his complex relation to the political and social structures of Geneva.

Calvin's emphasis on sanctification and discipleship in his description of the Christian life has occasionally evoked the charge of "legalism." He may claim that sanctification is the work of the Spirit and a manifestation of Christ's transforming grace, but through the years some of his critics have suggested that discipleship, as he describes it, seems less a gift than a requirement and a duty. That indictment neglects Calvin's repeated claim that sanctification is only one part of a twofold or double grace. To be bound to Christ by the Spirit, to receive forgiveness and new life in Christ, is to "cultivate blamelessness and purity of life." That aspect of transforming grace, however, is inseparable from and dialectically related to the other side of transforming grace—"being reconciled to God through Christ's blamelessness" and having "in heaven instead of a Judge a gracious Father"[21]—namely, justification by faith. Once again the influence of Augustine, Luther, and Melanchthon is clearly evident. While justification may not be for Calvin the article of faith by which the church stands or falls, he does describe it as "the main hinge on which religion turns." In other words, Christian faith does not "work"—the door is stuck—if the grace of Christ is a call to discipleship unrelated to Christ's justifying grace. If Calvin's description of sanctification is separated from what he says about Christ's justifying grace, sanctification might seem to be a duty, an obligation, something that must be done in order to receive God's grace, mercy, and forgiveness. The two—justification and sanctification—are distinct, but they also must not be separated, neither conceptually nor in daily Christian life. Separated from justification, sanctification may become a form of legalism or "works righteousness," and justification, separated from sanctification, may risk becoming a form of "cheap grace."

Calvin describes justification by faith as "the acceptance with which God receives us into his favor as righteous men." It consists of two parts: "the remission of sins and the imputation of Christ's righteousness."[22] By "imputation" Calvin means that sinners are not and cannot become by their own efforts righteous in themselves. They are righteous only in so far as they are "declared" or pronounced such by God because they are "in Christ." Christ alone is perfectly obedient to God the Father and hence Christ alone is righteous and is their righteousness. Christians, Calvin insisted, are justified not because they are themselves righteous, but because by the power of the Spirit they are in Christ, and God imputes Christ's righteousness to them. In and of themselves Christians are never anything before God but sinners. Their righteousness, to use Paul's expression, is a "free gift" God imputes to them as God's adopted children.

If God's grace is a free gift of the Spirit does that render human response, works of love and justice, unnecessary and superfluous? Like Augustine and Luther before him Calvin insists sinners cannot appeal to what they have done—including the act of faith itself—as the reason they should be recipients of God's grace. Works of love are the results, the "fruits," of God's free gift of grace rather than its cause. Through the centuries Protestant Christians have struggled with this basic distinction between justifying and sanctifying grace, between faith and works. Critical to understanding the distinction is Calvin's discussion of Christian freedom, which, not accidentally, immediately follows his interpretation of justification by faith.

Freedom and Law

Calvin describes Christian freedom as "a thing of prime necessity" and as "an appendage of justification" that is "of no little avail in understanding its power."[23] By freedom Calvin is referring neither to some innate quality of human existence nor to a general philosophical concept of freedom, but to a very particular form of freedom—the freedom Christians have in Jesus Christ, what Paul refers to in Galatians 5:1 as the freedom for which Christ sets us free. Calvin describes Christian freedom in three parts and in relation to God's law. As we noted in chapter 3, God's law first exposes the reality, if not the full extent, of human sinfulness. Second, it restrains evil in the civil order. Third, and principally, God's law shows forgiven sinners how they should live before God and with one another. It is important to keep these three "uses" of the law in mind in order to understand Calvin's description of the three parts of Christian freedom.[24]

First, in the context of God's justifying grace Christian freedom is freedom *from* the law. Because Christians "embrace God's mercy alone" they should look only to Christ and not to themselves in order to assure their anxious conscience. Righteousness is not to be found in the observance of the law, but only in Christ, and those who are in Christ are free from the law's indictment of sin.

Second, because their righteousness is no longer determined by their observance of the law Christians are free to obey God's will as that is revealed in God's commandments. Freed from the law by the righteousness of Christ, Christians are now free *for* the law, free to embrace the law joyously and to live according to it. Here Calvin embraces something of the spirit of Luther's description of Christian freedom as the paradox that "A Christian is a perfectly free lord of all, subject to none" and at the same time "A Christian is a perfectly dutiful servant of all, subject to all."[25] At this point Calvin's interpretation of the relation between the third use of God's law (the law shows forgiven sinners how they are to live) and the second part of Christian freedom (freedom for the law) is clear. Because they are "in Christ," Christians are free to embrace the law, not because their obedience to the law makes them righteous before God, but because God's Word, including the law of the covenant, is "a lamp to my feet and a light to my path" (Ps. 119:105) and, consequently, "I shall walk at liberty, for I have sought your precepts" (Ps. 119:45). Christian freedom is obedience, the freedom to obey God's Word.

The third part of Christian freedom concerns Christians' relations to the things of this world, things that the Stoics taught are in themselves "indifferent" (*adiaphora*). The things of this world, like the world itself, are gifts from God. Christians should receive them with thanksgiving and use them to glorify God. They should not let their consciences be consumed by questions such as whether it is more faithful to purchase sheets and shirts made out of hemp rather than linen or whether it is better to drink flat wine rather than sweet. Christians are free in regard to their use of the things of this world with one important caveat. Things "indifferent" must be used indifferently; "when they are coveted too greedily, when they are proudly boasted of, when they are lavishly squandered, things that were of themselves otherwise lawful are certainly defiled by these vices."[26] In other words if the material things of this world, which are themselves neither good nor evil, become obsessions that define a person's life, such that if one were to lose them life would no longer be worth living, then they are no longer things "indifferent," but idols that enslave.

Calvin offers three rules for how Christians should deal with earthly possessions, the third of which is that earthly things are given by the kindness of God, but they are given for our benefit and entrusted to us, "and we must one day render account of them."[27] The issue, then, is stewardship, and stewardship—the proper use of God's gifts—is an exercise of Christian freedom. Appealing to 1 Corinthians 10:23-24 and Paul's claim that "all things are lawful," Calvin argues Christians should use their freedom in such a manner that they "at all times seek after love and look toward the edification of our neighbor." That means Christian freedom should be used to enhance one's neighbor's life and to contribute to the common good. As opposed to other interpretations of freedom, Christian freedom is not the freedom to be and do anything, not the freedom "to be all that you can be." If Christian freedom does not help our neighbor,

Calvin insists, "then we should forego it." Christian freedom is not the freedom to acquire as much wealth as possible. It is a freedom that is inseparable from what he refers to as "the duties of love."[28] This interpretation of freedom may be sharply at odds with the way freedom is understood in "the land of the free and the home of the brave," where unlimited acquisition and consumption appear to be society's primary goals.

Perhaps the most important practice of Christian freedom for Calvin is prayer, a topic to which he devotes seventy pages in the final edition of the *Institutes*. Prayer is one of the primary benefits the Spirit provides to those who are in Christ. The Spirit not only reveals the promises of God's good will in Scripture and in preaching, but also "seals the witness of the gospel in our hearts" by training the Christian to appeal to God "in person concerning his promises in order to experience, where necessity so demands, that what they believed was not vain, although he had promised it in word alone."[29]

Prayer is an indispensable part of the Spirit's gift of life in Christ. The same Spirit who justifies sinners and makes them righteous by binding them to Christ also enables them to grow in their faith and transforms them by teaching them the practice of intimate conversation with God. Christians pray the prayer Christ teaches his disciples, not because it is a commandment or a duty or an obligation to do so, but because to live in Christ is to live freely before God by means of the first three petitions of the Lord's Prayer and to live freely with neighbors by means of the second three.

Election

The final topic in Calvin's portrait of the Christian life is perhaps the most controversial—the doctrine of election or predestination. The four chapters Calvin gives to this topic are roughly the same length as his one chapter on prayer, and yet over the centuries there have been many who considered his interpretation of election to be the centerpiece of his theology. It is not, but it is an important piece of it.

Calvin was not, of course, the first theologian to discover election as a prominent theme in the Bible. Augustine gave considerable attention to it, it was a persistent topic in medieval theology, and it was affirmed by many of the Protestant Reformers, including Luther and Bucer. Of particular importance is where Calvin locates the doctrine in the *Institutes*. It is not a separate topic in the first edition (1536) of the *Institutes* and in the second edition (1539) it is discussed in the same chapter as providence. In the final edition (1559), however, Calvin separated the two, placing providence at the conclusion to Book I (his discussion of God the creator) and predestination at the conclusion to Book III. Why did he separate them? They both affirm the sovereignty of God's gracious will. Wendel suggests that predestination concludes Book III "in order to show more clearly that it is in Christ that election takes place" and "to complete and illuminate the whole of the account of the Redemption."[30] In other words, one way to read Calvin on predestination is that it is not so much an explanation of who is redeemed and who is not as it is a confession, appropriate at the conclusion to a description of the Christian life, that reflects the experience of the Christian pilgrimage—namely, that the only way, finally, to account for a life lived in Christ, is that it was a life lived by God's grace alone. Election, then, is not so much an explanation as to why some people become Christians and others do not as it is a confession, best made in retrospect, at the conclusion of the Christian life, that the journey has not been about human faithfulness but about God's unrelenting pursuit and God's faithfulness, a confession that faith in Christ is not an achievement but a gift of God's Spirit.

The opening sentence of Calvin's discussion of predestination invites such an interpretation. "In actual fact," Calvin writes, "the covenant of life is not preached equally among all men, and among those to whom it is preached, it does not gain the same acceptance either constantly or in equal degree."[31] One suspects that "in actual fact" refers, at least in part, to Calvin's experience as a preacher and teacher for nearly thirty years in Geneva and Strasbourg, where he preached countless sermons and lectured frequently on the Bible. Perhaps he was puzzled why some people heard the gospel proclaimed and came to faith while others sat in church year after year and, as far as he could discern, gave no evidence of belief or regeneration. Was the reason to be found in the preacher and the quality of the sermon? If only he had worked longer, harder, more diligently would more of his listeners have heard the gospel and come to faith? "If it is plain," he observes, "that it [God's eternal election] comes to pass by God's bidding that salvation is freely offered to some while others are barred from access to it, great and difficult questions spring up. . . ."[32] And indeed the questions have sprung up. But given Calvin's premise that God's good will is to be found in all things, including the perplexing question of why some people become Christians and others do not, it is hardly a surprising conclusion for him to draw, especially since his theology was inextricably related to his work as a preacher and teacher.

Calvin argues for a twofold form of election. "We call predestation God's eternal decree, by which he compacted with himself what he willed to become of each man. For all are not created in equal condition: rather, eternal life is foreordained for some, eternal damnation for others."[33] Calvin does not evade or shy away from what he believes Scripture says. Whether one is predestined to election and salvation or to reprobation is due solely to God's good will and both—both election and damnation—are to the glory of God. He rejects a common misinterpretation of election that describes it simply as God's omniscience or foreknowledge of an individual's merits or lack thereof. In this view God elects those God knows "will not be unworthy of his grace" and rejects those "inclined to evil intention and ungodliness." Calvin appeals to Ephesians 1:4 and claims God's election takes place before creation, before the foundations of the world. Election is rooted not in what God knows but in what God wills. Repeatedly he invokes Genesis 25:23 and Romans 9:11-13, "I have loved Jacob, but I have hated Esau."

Not surprisingly Calvin's interpretation of predestination drew strenuous criticism from many of his contemporaries. A frequent objection concerned the interpretation of "the first sin." Did Adam sin of his own free will or did Adam sin because God willed it? A common response to this conundrum was to distinguish between what God wills and what God permits. God permitted Adam to sin but did not will him to do so; hence Adam remains culpable for his sin. But Calvin will have none of this. He does not back away from what he describes as God's "horrible decree." The distinction between God's will and God's permission, he argues, is false, because "why shall we say 'permission' unless it is because God so wills?"[34] God did not simply permit Adam to exercise his freedom; rather Adam fell "because the Lord had judged it to be expedient; why he so judged is hidden from us."[35] Furthermore, election is first and foremost about God's glory. God does not conform to some general concept of justice, just as God does not conform to some general notion of power or omnipotence. Calvin does not "advocate the fiction of 'absolute might' ";[36] God's power is the power to do what God does. And it is only that. It is not the power of "Could God create a rock so heavy God could not lift it?" So too God's justice is that which glorifies God. God's justice does not conform to "American justice" or to any other concept of justice. "Where you hear God's glory mentioned, think of his justice. For whatever deserves praise must be just."[37] Is God then the author of sin? In order to do justice (so to speak) to what Scripture says about God, Christians must affirm a paradox: Adam (and in him all humanity) "falls according as God's providence ordains, but he falls by his [Adam's] own fault."[38]

The objections to Calvin's interpretation of the doctrine of election were by no means limited to his contemporaries like Castellio, Bolsec, and Pighius. Numerous modern theologians, including Friedrich Schleiermacher in the nineteenth century and Karl Barth in the twentieth, have also disagreed with him. Calvin's claim that God ordains some to blessedness and others to damnation, Schleiermacher argued, seems to suggest that election is only about God's relation to individuals, forgetting that "no individual becomes anything whatever for himself, alone and apart from his place in the whole."[39] Instead of Calvin's categories of election and reprobation, Schleiermacher preferred the distinction between those who "are given perfect certainty of the divine decree for our blessedness" and those "in whom this consciousness has *not yet* developed."[40] The distinction between those who know God's redeeming grace in Jesus Christ and those who do not refers only to the state of affairs at any given moment in history. There are those who know God's grace and those who know it *not yet*, but who will, because "all belonging to the human race are eventually taken up into living fellowship with Christ."[41] Consequently, rather than a twofold fore-ordination or election Schleiermacher argues there is only a single divine fore-ordination that includes those who know God's grace in Jesus Christ and those who do not yet know it.

On the basis of Ephesians 1:4, Barth insists that God's election is always and only "in Christ." That means that there is only one who is truly elected by God and that is Jesus Christ who, following the logic of Chalcedon, is both the electing God and the elected human. Christ is the "second Adam" and just as all people are sinners in Adam so too all people are in Christ because Christ alone is both truly human and the one who assumes the sin of all sinners. Although he stops short of Schleiermacher's flat-footed universalism, Barth argues that Calvin did not fully pursue the logic of his position. Is there any assurance of election or is one left in the clutches of perpetual anxiety and terror? Calvin urges his readers to look to Christ and Barth agrees, because if they do so, they should not be anxious in regard to their election. If they are in communion with Christ, if when they look at him they see the embodiment of God's grace and good will, that alone, writes Calvin, is "a sufficiently clear and firm testimony that we have been inscribed in the book of life."[42]

Questions

1. Calvin says the sum of the Christian life is self-denial. What does he mean? Are people who have little or no self-esteem called to self-denial?

2. Are there certain things a Christian must do in order to be a Christian? If so, in what sense is the Christian free?

3. Schleiermacher and Barth disagreed with Calvin's interpretation of the doctrine of election. Whose position do you find the most compelling?

CHAPTER SEVEN

MOTHER CHURCH

I n the last edition (1559) of the *Institutes* Calvin devotes over five hundred pages, a third of the text, to the fourth and final book—his description of the church, the sacraments, and the church's relation to the state. This material may seem familiar to Protestant readers and perhaps not as interesting as his description of a world filled with angels and demons in which God's good and gracious will is involved in all things, a world in which God predestines some people to eternal life and others to reprobation. After five hundred years of Protestantism, Calvin's description of the church as that institution where the Word of God is purely preached and heard, the sacraments are properly administered, and believers are nurtured in their understanding and experience of faith is for many people all too familiar. And yet Christians have not always made the written and spoken Word the basis of their understanding of the church.

As the early Protestant Reformers began to restructure the church—not just its theology, but also its forms of worship and its internal organization and government—they wandered into new territory, and Calvin followed and borrowed from them, but his theology of the church (his "ecclesiology") was also shaped by the immediate demands he faced in Geneva. Calvin's ecclesiology, therefore, is found not only in what he writes about the church in the *Institutes*, in his commentaries on Scripture, and in his sermons, but also in his articles on the reorganization of the church in Geneva, in the deliberations of the Company of Pastors, and in the records or "registers" of the Consistory. What Calvin did in reforming the church is no less important than what he thought and wrote about it.

Means of Grace, Mother, and Nourishment

How does Calvin understand the church? Three of the many terms he uses to describe the church are particularly important. First, the title of Book IV of the *Institutes* is "The External Means or Aims by Which God Invites Us Into the Society of Christ and Holds Us Therein." The church is an "external means" or what Calvin also describes as one of those "outward helps" and "aids" by which Christians are united to Christ and participate in him (so that he no longer "remains outside of us" and "far from us") and thereby "are made the partakers of the salvation and eternal blessedness brought by him."[1] In other words, Book IV continues the basic theme of Book III—how the Holy Spirit binds Christians to Christ in order that they may receive Christ's benefits and be transformed by him. Book III describes how the Spirit does this in the internal regeneration of the individual Christian, and Book IV describes the Spirit's work in the external life of the Christian, in that "society of Christ" that is the church.

Second, Calvin describes the church by means of an image he borrows from several early church theologians—that of mother; "for those to whom he [God] is Father, the church may also be Mother."[2] Christians are forgiven sinners and as such they live by God's grace alone and are in the process of being sanctified by the Spirit. The Spirit gives them the gift of faith, but faith is not fixed and static but living and dynamic and must be nurtured and developed. The church is that society, that "mother," in which Christian faith, in both its individual and communal forms, is birthed, nursed, and developed. There is no other way to enter life—life in Christ—"unless this mother conceive us in her womb, give us birth, nourish us at her breast, and lastly, unless she keep us under her care and guidance until, putting off mortal flesh, we become like the angels."[3]

Calvin's third description of the church is implicit in the second, in his description of the church as mother. Reflecting the cultural assumptions of his day concerning gender roles, he understood mothers to have one primary responsibility—to nourish their children—and the church is that community where those who are in the process of becoming sanctified are fed, nourished, and developed.

All three of these descriptions point to an important feature of Calvin's interpretation of the church. The church is not significant in and of itself. It is significant because of what it does, because of the functions it performs. The church is not an end in itself, but an instrument, a means, for the glorification of God, the uniting of Christians with Christ, and the transformation of the world. The church is not itself a sacrament. It does not dispense, confer, or mediate grace. For Calvin there is only one Mediator, as we have seen in chapter 5, and that is Jesus Christ, and the church should not be confused with Christ. That means one does not believe in the church in the same way that one believes in the triune God. The church does not confer forgiveness and is not the object of faith. It is Christ alone who forgives sins and Christ alone in whom Christians should trust. What then do Christians mean then when they recite the Apostles' Creed and say, "I believe in the Holy Spirit, the holy catholic church, the communion of saints . . ."? There is no good reason, Calvin argues, to insert the preposition "in." Rather, we should say, "'I believe the church,' not '*in* the church.'"[4] In other words, Christians should not believe in the church in the sense that it is the church that is their "only comfort in life and in death" (the opening words of the Heidelberg Catechism of 1563); their only comfort is that they belong body and soul to Jesus Christ. However, it is in their life in the church, Calvin believes, that people learn to believe in God, and it is there that their faith in God is born, nurtured, and developed. It is more appropriate, therefore, not to say "I believe in the church," but to say "in the church I believe."[5]

Because the church is the external means by which the Spirit enables Christians to participate in Christ and to receive his benefits, because the principal benefit the church gives to Christians is faith, and because faith involves the heart as much as it does the mind, both of which must be nurtured and developed, Calvin concludes that it is indeed both "useful" and "necessary" to participate in the life of the church. It is a disaster to leave the church because to do so is to separate oneself from that "outward means" by which the Spirit sanctifies those who have been given justifying faith in Jesus Christ. The "necessity" of the church, therefore, is not that the church is important in and of itself. The church is necessary because God has chosen to use it to nurture those whom God has called to faith in Christ. Because of its function Christians cannot turn away from the church and develop their faith and their life in Christ elsewhere—either solely in their private lives or in some community other than the church. Although "God's power," writes Calvin, "is not bound to outward means,"[6] and God's Spirit is at work throughout the world, the church is that institution God has called into existence for the nurture and guidance of those God has chosen in Christ. Therefore, when Calvin writes, "it is always disastrous to leave the church,"[7] he does so not because life in the church is a good luck charm or an insurance policy against personal tragedy, but because the church is where Christians are in the process of being united to Christ, where faith is being born and nurtured.

Calvin's understanding of the church does not fit well in many modern Western societies where individuals are primary and communities are understood to be free, voluntary associations one can join and leave as one chooses. A "private Christian faith" or a "private spirituality" would be unintelligible to him, not because he believed it is a commandment or legal requirement to belong to a church, but because apart from the church faith soon withers and dies.

The Marks of the Church

If to be a faithful Christian entails life in the church, does it matter to which church one belongs? Are some churches more faithful to the gospel than others? In sixteenth-century Europe the question of what is and is not an authentic church was important. Calvin used two distinctions to describe an authentic church. The first, borrowed from Augustine, is a distinction between the visible and invisible church. The former, the visible church, consists of all those "spread over the earth who profess to worship one God and Christ." Unfortunately, in this visible church there are both those who have sincere faith and "many hypocrites who have nothing of Christ but the name and outward appearance."[8] How did Calvin know hypocrites were mingled with sincere believers in the church? On the one hand he believed that is what Scripture affirms, but, perhaps even more importantly, remember how he began his discussion of election in Book III. He appealed to his experience as a pastor and his discovery that the preaching of the Word is "not equally received in the church." The Spirit binds some people to Christ and gives them the gift of faith. These adopted, forgiven sinners live in the church by grace alone, and it is in the church that they begin their journey of sanctification—of self-denial, cross-bearing, and meditation on the future life. Others remain, for whatever reason, within the church but give little or no evidence they have truly and "efficaciously" heard the gospel. They continue to live unrepentant lives that contradict the faith they profess.

It is the visible church, Calvin insists, that is the external means of grace, the mother of faith, the society in which faith is born and nurtured, but only the invisible church consists of those who are "children of God by grace of adoption" (that is, those who are justified in Christ) "and true members of Christ by sanctification of the Holy Spirit."[9] This invisible church consists not only of saints now living "but all the elect from the beginning of the world" and is known only to God. It is beyond the wisdom or capability of any person to determine who within the visible church is truly elect and who is not.

Although Calvin's distinction between the visible and invisible church has not been without its critics, one can understand why he affirms it, both on the basis of his experience as a pastor and as a consequence of his doctrine of election. It is the Spirit who unites Christians to Christ, and this union includes their participation in Christ's body, the church, but life in Christ's church, like faith itself, is neither something inherited nor an inalienable right. It is just as much a mysterious, wondrous gift as is adoption. Christians do not so much "join up" with Christ and his church as they are "joined" to them. Life in the church, like life in Christ, is a great gift that occurs by grace alone. Consequently, the church is not the possession, the personal property, of any individual, family, or group, regardless of their wealth, social prominence, or longevity in the church. The church belongs to Christ alone.

Calvin's second distinction is between true and false churches. This is a distinction that should be understood, at least in part, in its historical context. In the mid-sixteenth century, significant changes were occurring in many churches. In those committed to reform, new forms of worship were emerging and the "order" and structure of the ministry were being revised. In the midst of this confusion, questions arose concerning what was and what was not a true and authentic church. Calvin did not reject the so-called Nicene marks of the church—that the church is one, holy, catholic, and apostolic—but he did carefully reinterpret what they meant. The holiness of the church, for example, did not mean that all its members (or any of them for that matter) were perfect in faithfulness and unblemished by sin; rather, they were "holy" because they were in the process of being conformed to Christ but had not yet reached that goal (and would not in this life).[10] In addition to these Nicene marks, Calvin followed Luther, Melanchthon, Bucer, and other early sixteenth-century reformers by identifying the distinguishing marks of the church as the proclamation of the Word and the administration of the sacraments. "Wherever we see the Word of God purely preached and heard, and the sacraments administered according to Christ's institution, there, it is not to be doubted, a church of God exists."[11] These two marks became the standard for testing whether a gathered community is truly a church. "If in Word and sacraments it has the order approved by the Lord, it will not deceive; let us, then, confidently pay to it the honor due to churches."[12]

Two things are significant about Calvin's "marks" of the church. First, they continue a central theme in his theology. The church is understood not so much ontologically (in terms of its being or what it is) as it is functionally (in terms of what it is called by God to do). The church does not confer God's grace and forgiveness. Only Christ, the sole Mediator between God and a sinful world, does that. The church is the body of Christ and as such it is the schoolhouse and the playground of the Spirit—where Christians are united to Christ and where faith is born, nurtured, and developed. Here the human words of the Bible become, for those the Spirit enables to read and hear them, the Word of God, and baptism and the Lord's Supper become visible signs and seals of God's grace in Christ.

Second, although Calvin does not name discipline as a third mark of the church, both in what he says about the church and even more importantly in his organization of the church in Geneva, he clearly considers it indispensable to any Christian community that aspires to be an authentic form of the body of Christ. In their life in the church Christians are moving toward the eschatological goal of the kingdom of heaven, which is "the only kingdom of righteousness."[13] Calvin devotes an entire chapter of Book IV to discipline in the church.[14] Discipline has three purposes: first, those who live lives that dishonor God must be banished from the church; second, in order to protect the faithful the wicked must be separated from them; and third, in order to bring unrepentant sinners to shame and repentance discipline must be exercised. Discipline, therefore, is simply an extension of the third (and principal) use of the law—to show freely forgiven sinners how they are to live before a righteous, merciful God.

Calvin put this understanding of discipline into practice in Geneva and it became a deeply divisive issue between himself and the rest of the Consistory on the one hand and on the other all those who were subject to discipline—that is, everyone in the city, including wealthy, prominent, and powerful people who were not accustomed to being disciplined by others. The various governing councils of the city worried that Calvin and the Consistory were usurping powers that properly belonged only to them. Whether the Consistory's only motive in its practice of discipline was to bring sinners to repentance and restoration to the life of the church is another matter, but discipline was not intended to be used in order to shame and humiliate, but in order that those who had gone astray might be brought back into the life of the church and continue their sanctification within it. Following Augustine, Calvin described discipline as "a severe mercy" that should bring "health rather than death to the body."[15]

This emphasis on discipline may be partially responsible for a common, widespread belief that Calvin emphasized God's judgment over God's mercy and grace and turned the gospel into a new form of legalism. This misinterpretation may arise from the abuse of the third use of the law and church discipline by many Christian denominations influenced by Calvin. Most have something like a Directory for Discipline in their "polity" or government, but sometimes they have forgotten that discipline is not for the sake of punishment but for repentance and restoration. The line between the two can be thin.

What Calvin means by the positive role "discipline" plays is perhaps clearer when he discusses fasting in the Christian life, by which he does not mean simply giving up food, but "another sort of fasting, temporary in character, when we withdraw something from the normal regimen of living, either for one day or for a definite time, and pledge ourselves to a tighter and more severe restraint in diet than ordinarily."[16] Such a discipline helps Christians develop what Calvin believed to be important features of a godly life—frugality and sobriety.

Calvin's theology is clearly reflected in the Scottish Confession of 1560, which declares that not only the pure preaching of the Word and the proper administration of the sacraments but also the exercise of discipline are the three marks of the church. Are there, however, only three marks of the church? There is not unanimity among Reformed churches concerning the precise number of marks of the church. The Bohemian Confession of 1570, for example, lists five marks of the church. In addition to the preaching of the Word, the administration of the sacraments, and the exercise of discipline, it adds bearing the cross and the practice of poverty, two themes prominent in Calvin's description of the Christian life.[17] Regardless of the number of the marks, what is significant about these Christian communities that trace their theology to Calvin is that they interpret the church primarily in terms of the tasks and functions to which God calls it and not as something that is important in and of itself.

Sacraments

Calvin's church is a "Christian society" in which the Word is preached and the sacraments are properly administered. Both tasks are to be performed by ministers duly called by God and confirmed by the voice of the church, but the efficacy of both tasks—the preaching of the Word and the administering of the sacraments—depends solely on the work of the Holy Spirit. It is the Spirit who enables sinful people to read God's Word in scripture and to hear it in the sermon; it is also the Spirit who uses the water of baptism and the bread and wine of the Lord's Supper to seal the promises of God declared in the Word upon the hearts of those who receive the sacraments. For Calvin the sacraments are distinct but inseparable from the Word. Word and sacrament belong together, and, like the church itself, are the external means by which the Spirit binds Christians to Christ and enables them to have new life in him.

The influence of Augustine is obvious in Calvin's discussion of the sacraments. He invokes Augustine's definition of them as "a visible form of an invisible grace." Echoing the language he used to define faith, Calvin describes them as "an outward sign by which the Lord seals on our consciences the promises of his good will toward us in order to sustain the weakness of our faith." They are the means by which "we in turn attest our piety toward him in the presence of the Lord and of his angels and before men." Or more succinctly they are "a testimony of divine grace toward us, confirmed by an outward sign, with mutual attestation of our piety toward him."[18] The sacraments, therefore, are a twofold form of testimony. They are a testimony on God's part of "divine grace toward us," and they are a testimony of faith in God by those who participate in them.

Calvin says a great deal in these brief definitions of sacrament. First, the sacraments refer or point to something. They are visible, tangible signs of God's promise of gracious good will to the world. Second, they are not only signs but also seals of God's promises of grace given in both the written words of Scripture and the spoken words of proclamation. Hence Word and sacrament are reciprocally related. The one should not be separated from the other. A sacrament "is never without a preceding promise but is joined to it as a sort of appendix, with the purpose of confirming and sealing the promise itself, and of making it more evident to us and in a sense ratifying it."[19]

Third, not only do the sacraments presuppose the Word but they also presuppose faith. They are an aid, a gift from God in order to sustain the weakness of faith. In this sense the sacraments, no less than the Word, are "instruments" of God's grace. They nurture and confirm faith, but ordinarily they do so differently than does the Word. They engage the eye more than the ear. Borrowing from Augustine, Calvin describes sacraments as not a spoken but a visible Word. They are "mirrors in which we may contemplate the riches of God's grace, which he lavishes upon us."[20] They confirm faith "when they set before our eyes the good will of our Heavenly Father toward us, by the knowledge of whom the whole firmness of our faith stands fast and increases in strength."[21] Unlike the proclamation of the Word, the sacraments represent God's promises "as painted in a picture from life."[22]

Fourth, not only do the sacraments presuppose faith, but also piety, for there is no true faith unless it is accompanied by piety, because what is affirmed by the mind must also be longed for in the heart. Finally, the sacraments are not efficacious in and of themselves. Calvin rejected what he considered a superstitious or magical interpretation of the sacraments, one he believed to be widespread in the Catholicism of his day. The sacraments do not have "some secret force or other perpetually seated in them by which they are able to promote or confirm faith by themselves."[23] Just as it is the Spirit who binds Christians to Christ and in so doing gives them the gift of faith, so it is the Spirit alone who makes baptism and the Lord's Supper efficacious.

Baptism, therefore, is a sign of "initiation" into the life of the church and of "engrafting" into Christ. It is a threefold sign. First, it is a "token" of the cleaning, washing, and purging of sin by Christ's sacrificial blood. Second, it "shows us our mortification in Christ, and new life in him."[24] Third, it is a sign that those baptized are united with Christ in his death and resurrection and share in his "benefits" or blessings. The sign must be in the name of the triune God because although baptism is "in Christ" and "he is the proper object of baptism," the Father is the cause and the Holy Spirit "the effect of our purgation and our regeneration."[25]

Because Christ is the Mediator of the covenant, Calvin understands baptism to be "foreshadowed" in God's history with Israel. The story in Exodus of God's deliverance of Israel from bondage in Egypt and the rite of circumcision are precursors of Christian baptism. Baptism is "put in place of circumcision in order to represent to us what circumcision signified to the Jews of old."[26] The inseparability of the Old and New Testaments is important for Calvin because he is fighting on two fronts. On the one hand he rejects the Roman Catholic position that baptism sets Christians free from original sin and restores them to Adam's original righteousness. Furthermore, because no one is saved simply by being baptized, they should not delay their baptisms, as many did in Calvin's day, until they were near death in order to make sure that their balance sheets were in good order and they did not perish in a state of sin. For Calvin baptism is a sign and a seal of God's promise of grace already fulfilled in Christ, and, therefore, closely linked in the logic or grammar of Calvin's theology to the doctrine of justification. Baptized Christians are not restored to an original righteousness, but, because they are united to Christ, become God's adopted children and receive the benefit of the "imputation" of his righteousness.

Calvin argues against the Roman Catholic understanding of baptism and also against Anabaptist interpretations, such as those of Balthasar Hubmaier (1485–1528) and the Schleitheim Confession of 1527, as well. Of the two chapters on baptism in the 1559 *Institutes*, the second, chapter 16, is Calvin's defense of infant baptism, and is nearly twice as long as the preceding chapter on the meaning of baptism. Despite its length he describes chapter 16 as "an appendix" to chapter 15 (which it was in the 1536 *Institutes*), occasioned by the attacks of "certain frantic spirits" on infant baptism. Anabaptists had several objections to infant baptism, but two were particularly important. First, they found no basis for the practice of infant baptism in the New Testament, and, second, infant baptism appeared to separate the sacrament from the confession of faith by the person being baptized, and thus separated baptism and discipleship, making baptism not a participation in Christ's death and resurrection but a celebration of cheap grace.

Calvin responds at some length to these Anabaptist objections, but not very successfully. He makes two kinds of arguments—one based on the practice of baptism in the New Testament and the other based on the theological meaning of baptism. In the first, because he argues theology should be derived from the Bible rather than from Christian tradition, he is hard-pressed to find examples of the practice of infant baptism in the churches of the New Testament. In the second, he argues that baptism takes the place of circumcision in the Old Testament even though there are few New Testament texts that correlate baptism with circumcision. He also appeals repeatedly to Matthew 19:13-15 (Jesus' command that the disciples not prevent children from being brought to him), acknowledging that in this text Jesus says nothing to his disciples about baptizing the children, but arguing, unconvincingly, that if "it is right for infants to be brought to Christ, why not also to be received into baptism, the symbol of our communion and fellowship with Christ?"[27] In response to the "silly objection" that there is no evidence in the New Testament of "a single infant's ever being baptized," Calvin argues that "because infants are not excluded when mention is made of a family's being baptized, who in his senses can reason from this that they were not baptized?"[28] By that logic one can imagine all kinds of things in a family that become eligible for baptism. Even more remarkably, he invokes "the rule of faith," the creeds of the early church—that is, church tradition—and appeals "to the purpose for which it [baptism] was instituted." Baptism's purpose means "it is just as appropriate to infants as to older persons."[29]

In the twentieth century Calvin's position on infant baptism has been disputed not only by theologians from Anabaptist traditions, but also by Reformed theologians such as Karl Barth and Jürgen Moltmann. Calvin could not have foreseen some of their objections to infant baptism because it would have been impossible for him to imagine a twentieth-century post-Christian Europe and a largely secular culture. Questions about the meaning of discipleship and mission in this new situation have led several theologians to question whether infant baptism remains what it originally was for Calvin—a sign and a seal of God's prevenient grace—or whether it has now become simply a cultural ritual and as such disconnected from the call to discipleship.

Calvin's interpretation of the Lord's Supper or Eucharist emerged in the midst of sixteenth-century controversies at least as heated and as widespread as those surrounding baptism. He was no less indebted to Augustine's theory of signs and how they signify than many of the other figures in these debates. On this topic, like so many others, the question was not whether Augustine was relevant, but how he should be interpreted. Just as Calvin had insisted Christ's two natures be distinguished but not separated, so too he argued that the sign and the matter it signifies must be understood the same way.

That principle was the basis of his objection to both Roman Catholic and Zwinglian interpretations of the Lord's Supper. He believed the Catholic position of transubstantiation—that the substance, but not the "accidents," of the bread and wine are transformed into the body and blood of Jesus—collapsed the distinction between the sign and matter (that is, Christ), with the consequence that the bread and wine were understood to have "some sort of secret powers with which one nowhere reads that God has endowed them." For Catholics, if the Christian was not in a state of mortal sin then the sacraments would "justify and confer grace." This Catholic affirmation of the objective efficacy of the sacraments, *ex opera operato* (they confer grace simply by being properly performed), made them necessary for salvation. For Calvin the sacraments were important, even necessary to sustain faith, but not necessary for salvation.

On the other hand, Calvin objected to the Zwinglian position because it separated the sign and the matter it signified. For Zwingli the bread and the wine point to the saving event of the cross in the past and the faith of Christians in the present, but Christ is not present in the bread and wine, and, consequently, there is no relation between sign and what it signifies.

Calvin developed an interpretation of Christ's presence in the Lord's Supper between these two positions, between the objectivity of the Catholics and the subjectivity of the Zwinglians. The bread and wine on the one hand and Christ's body and blood on the other are distinct but also inseparable. They are united and in this union Christians receive the primary benefit of the Lord's Supper—union with Christ that sustains and nourishes their faith. How does this union occur? Calvin acknowledges that here he bumps up against mystery (*sacramentum* is the Latin translation for the Greek *mysterion*) that is beyond the reach and understanding of reason. Calvin writes that he is not ashamed to admit that how this happens "is a secret too lofty for either my mind to comprehend or my words to declare," and "to speak more plainly, I rather experience than understand it."[30] Just as the principal work of the Holy Spirit is to unite Christians to Christ by giving them the gift of faith, so too in the Lord's Supper it is the Spirit who unites those who participate faithfully in the sacrament with Christ by lifting them into his presence. Christ is resurrected and ascended and is not "locally" present in the bread and the wine but in the words of the Apostles' Creed "sits at the right hand of God the Father." It is the Spirit who gives Christians faith and enables them to commune with the risen and ascended Christ and to be nourished and fed by him. It is by the work of the Spirit that Christ is present in the Lord's Supper and it is the Spirit who enables Christians to partake of his body and blood.

Brian Gerrish has argued there are two reasons why Calvin's interpretation of the Lord's Supper is important for understanding his theology. First, more so than elsewhere in his theology, here we clearly see Calvin's personal piety—a piety centered on grace and gratitude—and perhaps also something of Calvin's own Christian experience. Second, this material discloses "the eucharistic shape of Calvin's entire theology."[31] For Calvin the Lord's Supper is the free gift of God's grace in Jesus Christ. The Holy Spirit makes the bread and wine "efficacious" by giving Christians faith and enabling them to commune with Christ and to be fed and nourished by him.[32] Not just the Lord's Supper but Christian faith in its entirety, as Calvin described it, is about God's grace and Christian gratitude.

Questions

1. Calvin describes the marks of the church as the preaching and hearing of the Word and the proper administration of the sacraments. Are these marks sufficient to

identify an authentic form of the church? Or are other marks—such as mission and commitment to the poor—also necessary?

2. Should the church baptize the infants of Christians? If so, why is this not "cheap grace"? If not, why is this not "works righteousness"?

3. In what sense, if any, is Christ present in the Lord's Supper?

CHAPTER EIGHT

CALVIN AND HIS CHILDREN

Calvin and Calvinism

Calvin belongs in any series on "the pillars of theology" because of his enduring significance. His theology did not end with his burial in an unmarked grave in Geneva's cemetery. His influence extends beyond the sixteenth century and is visible in theologians as diverse as the English Puritan William Ames in the seventeenth century, the American Jonathan Edwards in the eighteenth century, Friedrich Schleiermacher in early nineteenth-century Berlin, and Karl Barth in twentieth-century Switzerland.

Nor was Calvin's influence limited geographically to Geneva and Reformed churches in his native France. He had a direct impact on the emergence of Reformed theology in Scotland (Knox twice came to Geneva to hear Calvin lecture), Germany, Holland, the Puritans in England, the Waldensians in Italy, and movements in Poland and Transylvania.[1]

In the nineteenth and twentieth centuries Reformed churches in the United States and Western Europe undertook missions in the rest of the world and the Reformed tradition spread globally—in Asia, Africa, the Middle East, and Central and South America. The global reality of the Reformed tradition today is found in organizations such as the World Alliance of Reformed Churches, consisting of more than two hundred denominations. In the second half of the twentieth century non-Western Reformed churches began to struggle with questions about the meaning of the gospel in their own contexts. It gradually became apparent to many of them that Western interpretations of Christian faith (and of Reformed faith in particular) did not address their distinctive social histories and cultural experiences. In the last half of the twentieth century they began to write their own confessions in ways that reflected their histories and cultures. This "contextualization" of the Reformed tradition has included discussions of the relation between it and liberation theology in South Africa, Marxism in Cuba, minjung theology in Korea, and the emergence of feminist theology.[2]

Perhaps because Calvin believed that everything in Geneva, not just religious life, should be conformed to the Word of God, his influence has extended not only beyond the sixteenth century and the theological issues of his time, but to the development of culture, economics, and politics in the rest of the world as well. Historians and social scientists have found Calvin's fingerprints everywhere. One of the best known examples is Max Weber's *The Protestant Ethic and the Spirit of Capitalism* (1905), which attempted to correlate Calvinist themes such as election, vocation, and frugality with the emergence and development of capitalism.[3] Similarly, Michael Walzer's *The*

Revolution of the Saints: a Study in the Origins of Radical Politics (1965) argued that "it was the Calvinists who first switched the emphasis of political thought from the prince to the saint (or the band of saints) and then constructed a theoretical justification for independent political action." And it was through these saints—Genevan, Huguenot, Dutch, Scottish, and Puritan—that "conscience and work entered the political world together" and "formed the basis for the new politics of revolution."[4]

Although some of Calvin's ideas, appropriated in different forms of Calvinism, may have tilled the soil for the growth of movements such as free market capitalism and liberal democracy, that does not mean there is a direct, causal relation between Calvin and the modern world. Walzer's caution about the "putative connection of Calvin and capitalism" also applies to any attempt to make seventeenth-century Puritan saints the founders of liberal democracy. "The moral discipline of the saints can be interpreted as the historical conditioning of the capitalist man; but the discipline was not itself capitalist."[5] It is hardly surprising, therefore, that "virtually all the modern world has been read into Calvinism: liberal politics and voluntary association; capitalism and the social discipline upon which it rests; bureaucracy with its systematic procedures and its putatively diligent and devoted officials; and finally all the routine forms of repression, joylessness, and unrelaxed aspiration. . . . [T]he faith of the brethren, and especially of the Puritan brethren, has been made the source or cause or first embodiment of the most crucial elements of modernity."[6]

But just as it would be a mistake to draw a causal connection between Calvin's theology and the emergence of free market capitalism and liberal democracy, so too it would be misleading to make Calvin responsible for all the historical horrors inflicted on the world by his heirs. To be sure Calvinists in the nineteenth and twentieth centuries have been complicit in the creation and support of institutions such as slavery in the United States, apartheid in South Africa, the spread of colonialism in the mission fields of the non-Western world, and the development of an American foreign policy of "manifest destiny." Unfortunately, some of Calvin's heirs seem to have been more embarrassed by his role in Servetus's death than they have by their involvement in slavery, apartheid, and colonialism. These latter horrors, however, reflect Calvin's theology in one important respect. They are an all-too-vivid reminder of the power of sin to deceive and corrupt both individuals and social and political institutions.

Calvin and Politics

It is significant that the *Institutes* begins and ends with discussions about Christian faith and politics. Calvin's life in Geneva was an embodied conviction that Christian faith cannot be a private matter, unrelated to public, social existence. He believed that all of life, personal and communal, should be conformed to God's Word. The first edition (1536) of the *Institutes* begins with a preface in the form of an "address" to Francis I, "Most Christian King of the French," written in the immediate aftermath of two important events. First, in the Placards affair of October 18, 1534, handbills attacking the Catholic Mass were distributed throughout France, including Francis's bedroom. Severe repression in France followed and many people in the reform movement were thrown into prison or killed, while others, including Calvin, fled France for safety elsewhere. Second, in June 1535, violent, millennial Anabaptists seized Münster (in what we know today as Germany) and established a theocracy that was soon surrounded by military forces and degenerated into polygamy and enormous human suffering. It is in that context that Calvin wrote to Francis explaining that his sole purpose in writing the *Institutes* was "to transmit certain rudiments by which those who are touched with any zeal for religion might be shaped to true godliness."[7] He wrote to assure Francis that he had nothing to fear from the small Reformed church in France that "has either been wasted with cruel slaughter or banished into exile, or so overwhelmed by threats and fears that it dare not even open its mouth."[8] It was "fraud," Calvin insisted, to accuse the movement for church reform of "treason and villainy," as though its goal were "to wrest the scepters from the hands of kings, to cast down all courts and judgments, to subvert all orders and civil governments, to disrupt the peace and quiet of the people, to abolish all laws, to scatter all lordships and possessions—in short, to turn everything upside down!"[9]

The final edition (1559) of the *Institutes* also begins with Calvin's letter to Francis I, but it concludes with a discussion of the role of civil government. In the first edition this material was part of Calvin's discussion of the nature of Christian freedom. Does Christian freedom mean that Christians are antinomians—that they have been set free from courts, laws, and magistrates? Not so, because Christ's spiritual kingdom and "future eternal life" on the one hand and civil government and "this present earthly life" on the other are distinct but not unrelated. The purpose of civil government is "to cherish and protect the outward worship of God, to defend sound doctrine of piety and the position of the church, to adjust our life to the society of men, to form our social behavior to civil righteousness, to reconcile us with one another, and to promote general peace and tranquility."[10] Unlike some of the radical Anabaptists of his day, Calvin did not consider civil government "a thing polluted," something "unworthy of us," and unrelated to Christian life, but a "help" along the way as Christians, surrounded by the insolence and wickedness of evil people, travel "to the true fatherland." Civil government has its appointed end within God's providence and to consider doing away with it because "there ought to be such great perfection in the church of God that its government should suffice for law" is "outrageous barbarity."[11] Government exists to rightly establish religion, to prevent idolatry, to maintain public peace, to protect private property, and to provide "that a public manifestation of religion may exist among Christians, and that humanity be maintained among men."[12]

There are, Calvin writes, three parts to civil government: the magistrate, the laws, and the people "who are governed by the laws and obey the magistrate."[13] The magistrate is God's representative, vice regent, and vicar, and has been called by God to that office and "invested with divine authority."[14] Consequently, the magistrate has "a jurisdiction bestowed by God," and holds an office worthy of honor and even reverence. Just as Calvin does not want the creator confused with creation, so too the will of God must not be confused with the will of the magistrate. Nonetheless, because God calls magistrates to their offices, to resist them is to resist God. Even if the magistrate is wicked and rules unjustly, Calvin considers resistance impermissible because Scripture provides numerous examples of God giving Israel corrupt rulers in order that they may serve God's larger purposes. For Calvin it is God who calls magistrates to their office and God alone who overturns them.

In the final two sections of the final chapter of the *Institutes* Calvin provides an exception to the obedience he argues Christians owe the magistrate. Unjust, even unwise and immoral behavior by the magistrate is not sufficient cause for people to resist their rulers because "the correction of unbridled despotism is the Lord's to avenge."[15] However, obedience to the magistrate must never entail disobedience to God "to whose will the desires of all kings ought to be subject, to whose decrees all their commands ought to yield, to whose majesty their scepters ought to be submitted."[16] In other words, not just in the church but in civil government as well, God and God alone is the final, sole authority. If magistrates command anything contrary to what God wills "let it go unesteemed." Repeatedly Calvin cites biblical texts such as Daniel 6 (Daniel's refusal to obey King Darius's decrees forbidding prayer to anyone other than himself) and 1 Kings 12:25-33 (Israel's apostasy in worshiping King Jeroboam's golden calf at Bethel and Dan). If faced with a decision whether to disobey God or a magistrate, Calvin cites the Apostle Peter—"'We must obey God rather than men' (Acts 5:29)" and "suffer anything rather than turn aside from piety."[17]

Calvin's understanding of civil government will seem strange to many readers in modern, Western democracies who do not believe those who hold political office are called by God to do so. Sixteenth-century Geneva was not a modern democracy. Calvin's personal preference among possible forms of government was "a system composed of aristocracy and democracy," because political power should not be vested in a single person and it is "safer and more bearable for a number to exercise government."[18] In his recognition of the danger of unrestricted political power Calvin may have been a forerunner of modern democratic developments, but his acceptance of aristocracy and social hierarchy suggest he may have been closer to Cicero's *De Legibus* (*On the Laws*) than he was to Thomas Jefferson's *Declaration of Independence*.

Although Calvin clearly believed that Christians should understand their rulers as called by God to their positions of authority, he did allow for the possibility for resistance if obedience to the magistrate meant disobedience to God. That principle of God's prerogative was not lost on numerous Calvinists over the centuries who have resisted governments whose rule they considered not only unjust but also contrary to God's will.

Calvin's Dialectics

Many commentators have noted various tensions in Calvin's theology. William Bouwsma describes Calvin as "a singularly anxious man" whose anxiety is reflected in his use of images such as the abyss and the labyrinth. On the one hand there is Calvin the philosopher who seems fearful of chaos, disorder, and non-being—the abyss—and who desperately craves intelligibility, order, and certainty. On the other hand there is Calvin the rhetorician and humanist, "a revolutionary in spite of himself," who dreads "entrapment in a labyrinth" and who celebrates "the paradoxes and mystery at the heart of existence."[19] These tensions in Calvin, however, assume other forms as well. On the one hand Calvin describes the Bible as the oracles of God and this "side" of Calvin can be understood as the basis for something like a position of the verbal inerrancy of Scripture. But on the other hand, the Bible becomes God's Word only when the Holy Spirit enables sinful humans to hear, read, and discern it as such. On the one hand, Calvin fears anarchy and understands magistrates to be invested with divine authority. On the other hand, if magistrates demand their subjects do that which is contrary to God's will they should no longer be "esteemed," but should be actively resisted.

These and numerous other examples reflect tensions and paradoxes in Calvin. Their significance is that, for want of a better term, the "conservative" side of Calvin—which fears disorder and anarchy and yearns for order and structure, a fixed reading of the Bible, and divinely established political authority—always stands in tension with Calvin's "liberalism," with his faith in a living God who transcends human authorities and institutions, who continues to speak in Scripture in new and surprising ways, and who alone among all authorities is to be obeyed and worshiped.

How should these dialectical tensions in Calvin be understood? One could argue that each side, when separated from the other, leads to a disastrously distorted form of Christian faith. Those American Presbyterians and South African Dutch Reformed Christians who constructed and supported social systems of slavery and apartheid are perhaps examples of what happens when a fear of change turns into an idolatry of the established order. On the other hand, the triumph of secularism, the accommodation of faith to free market economies, and the loss of a sense of Christian identity among Reformed churches in Western Europe and North America is perhaps an example of what happens when Christian freedom ceases to be the obedience of discipleship and becomes an ideology of self-gratification. Neither was what Calvin intended.

Calvin has many children, including those who gathered at Barmen in Germany in 1934 in the face of the horror that became Nazi Germany and who confessed before God and the world that "Jesus Christ, as he is attested for us in Holy Scripture, is the one Word of God which we have to hear and which we have to trust and obey in life and in death." These children of Calvin rejected the notion that a church faithful to the gospel could "abandon the form of its message and order to its own pleasure or to changes in prevailing ideological and political convictions."[20] Nearly fifty years later, during September-October, 1982, other descendents of Calvin gathered at Belhar in the Republic of South Africa and rejected any doctrine that "sanctions in the name of the gospel or the will of God the forced separation of people on the grounds of race and color and thereby in advance obstructs and weakens the ministry and experience of reconciliation in Christ."[21]

Were those who gathered at Barmen and Belhar Calvin's good children, his true heirs? Did they successfully hold together the tensions in his theology, tensions rooted in the gospel itself, tensions that others—the conservatives in their idolatrous concern for social order and the liberals in their commitment to a vacuous freedom—destroyed? The deepest tension in Calvin's theology is something he derives from the Bible—the recognition that idolatry casts a long shadow in the lives of all people, even among the saints of the church, and that their only hope, and the hope of all people, is God's gracious good will in Jesus Christ.

Questions

1. What, if anything, is there in Calvin's theology that accounts for its survival in twentieth-first-century theology and its continuing influence in non-Western churches?

2. Given his letter to Francis I, assuring the king that the movement of reform was no threat to his political rule, was Calvin a political conservative? Or is his position in the last chapter of the *Institutes* that rulers must not compel Christians to disobey God the basis for a politics of radical resistance?

3. If there is a permanently destabilizing principle in Christian faith—the God whose will is to transform all things—is there anything, including faith itself, that is not open to God's reformation?

BIBLIOGRAPHY

I. Writings

Ioannis Calvini Opera quae supersunt Omnia. Eds. Wilhelm Baum, Edward Cunitz, and Edward Reuss. 59 vols. in *Corpus Reformatorum*, vols. 29–87. Brunswick: C.A. Schwetschke and Son, 1863–1900.

Ioannis Calvini Opera Selecta. Eds. Peter Barth, Wilhelm Niesel, and Doris Scheuner. 5 vols. Munich: Chr. Kaiser Verlag, 1926–1952.

De Greef, Wulfert. *The Writings of John Calvin: An Introductory Guide*. Exp. ed. Trans. Lyle D. Bierma. Louisville: Westminster John Knox Press, 2008.

II. Translations

Bonnet, Jules. *Letters of John Calvin*. 4 vols. New York: Burt Franklin Reprints, 1972.

Calvin, John. *Calvin's Ecclesiastical Advice*. Trans. Mary Beaty and Benjamin W. Farley. Louisville: Westminster John Knox Press, 1991.

———. *Calvin's New Testament Commentaries. A New Translation*. 12 vols. Eds. David W. Torrance and Thomas F. Torrance. Grand Rapids: William B. Eerdmans Publishing Company, 1963.

———. *The Commentaries of John Calvin*. 46 vols. Edinburgh: Calvin Translation Society, 1843–1855. Grand Rapids: Eerdmans, 1948–1950.

———. *Institutes of the Christian Religion*. Ed. John T. McNeill. Trans. Ford Lewis Battles. 2 vols. Library of Christian Classics, vols. 20 and 21. Philadelphia: Westminster Press, 1960.

———. *Institution of the Christian Religion*. Trans. Ford Lewis Battles. Atlanta: John Knox Press, 1975.

———. *Instruction in Faith (1537)*. Trans. Paul T. Fuhrmann. Louisville: Westminster John Knox Press, 1977.

———. *Theological Treatises*. Trans. with Introduction and Notes by John K. S. Reid. Library of Christian Classics. Philadelphia: Westminster Press, 1954.

———. *Tracts and Treatises on the Reformation of the Church*. Trans. Henry Beveridge. 3 vols. Grand Rapids: Eerdmans, 1958.

III. Biographies

Bouwsma, William J. *John Calvin: A Sixteenth Century Portrait*. New York: Oxford University Press, 1988.

Cottret, Bernard. *Calvin: A Biography*. Trans. M. Wallace McDonald. Grand Rapids: Eerdmans, 2000.

Doumergue, Émile. *Jean Calvin, les hommes et les choses de son temps*. 7 vols. Lausanne: G. Bridel: 1899–1927.

Ganoczy, Alexandre. *The Young Calvin*. Trans. David L. Foxgrover and Wade Provo. Philadelphia: Westminster Press, 1987.

McGrath, Alister E. *A Life of John Calvin: A Study in the Shaping of Western Culture.* Oxford: Blackwell, 1990.

Parker, T. H. L. *John Calvin: A Biography.* Philadelphia: Westminster Press, 1975.

Walker, Williston. *John Calvin: The Organiser of Reformed Protestantism (1509–1564).* Bibliographical introduction by John T. McNeill. New York: Schocken Books, 1969.

Wendel, François. *John Calvin: The Origins and Development of His Religious Thought.* Trans. Philip Mairet. New York: Harper & Row, 1963.

IV. Calvin in Geneva

Graham, W. Fred. *The Constructive Revolutionary: John Calvin and His Socio-Economic Impact.* Richmond: John Knox Press, 1971.

Innes, William C. *Social Concern in Calvin's Geneva.* Allison Park, Penn.: Pickwick Publications, 1983.

Kingdon, Robert M. *Adultery and Divorce in Calvin's Geneva.* Cambridge: Harvard University Press, 1995.

———. *Geneva and the Coming of the Wars of Religion in France, 1555–1563.* Geneva: Librairie Droz, 1956.

Kingdon, Robert M., Thomas A. Lambert, and Isabella M. Watts, eds. *Registers of the Consistory of Geneva in the Time of Calvin.* Trans. M. Wallace McDonald. Vol. 1 (1542–1544). Grand Rapids: Eerdmans, 2000.

Monter, E. William. *Calvin's Geneva.* New York: John Wiley & Sons, 1967.

Naphy, William G. *Calvin and the Consolidation of the Genevan Reformation.* Manchester and New York: Manchester University Press, 1994.

Steinmetz, David C. *Calvin in Context.* New York: Oxford University Press, 1995.

Wallace, Ronald S. *Calvin, Geneva and the Reformation.* Edinburgh: Scottish Academic Press, 1988.

V. Calvin's Theology

Barth, Karl. *The Theology of John Calvin.* Trans. Geoffrey W. Bromiley. Grand Rapids: Eerdmans, 1995.

Battles, Ford Lewis. *Interpreting John Calvin.* Ed. Robert Benedetto. Grand Rapids: Baker Books, 1996.

Dowey, Edward. *The Knowledge of God in Calvin's Theology.* New York: Columbia University Press, 1952.

Edmondson, Stephen. *Calvin's Christology.* Cambridge: Cambridge University Press, 2004.

Gamble, Richard, ed. *Articles on Calvin and Calvinism—A Fourteen-volume Anthology of Scholarly Articles.* 14 vols. New York: Garland Publishing Co., 1992.

George, Timothy, ed. *John Calvin and the Church: A Prism of Reform.* Louisville: Westminster John Knox, 1990.

Gerrish, B. A. *Grace and Gratitude: The Eucharistic Theology of John Calvin.* Minneapolis: Fortress Press, 1993.

————, ed. *Reformatio Perennis: Essays on Calvin and the Reformation in Honor of Ford Lewis Battles*. Pittsburgh: The Pickwick Press, 1981.

————. "Theology Within the Limits of Piety Alone: Schleiermacher and Calvin's Doctrine of God" in *Reformatio Perennis: Essays on Calvin and the Reformation in Honor of Ford Lewis Battles*. Ed. B. A. Gerrish. Pittsburgh: The Pickwick Press, 1981, 67–87.

————. "'To the Unknown God': Luther and Calvin on the Hiddenness of God" in *The Old Protestantism and the New: Essays on the Reformed Heritage*. Chicago: The University of Chicago Press, 1982, 138–49.

Hesselink, I. John. *Calvin's First Catechism: A Commentary*. Trans. Ford Lewis Battles. Louisville: Westminster John Knox Press, 1997.

Jansen, John F. *Calvin's Doctrine of the Word of Christ*. London: James Clarke and Co., 1956.

McKim, Donald K., ed. *The Cambridge Companion to John Calvin*. Cambridge: Cambridge University Press, 2004.

Muller, Richard A. *After Calvin: Studies in the Development of a Theological Tradition*. New York: Oxford University Press, 2003.

————. *The Unaccommodated Calvin: Studies in the Foundation of a Theological Tradition*. Oxford: Oxford University Press, 2000.

Neuser, Wilhelm H., ed. *Calvinus Sacrae Scripturae Professor: Calvin as Confessor of Holy Scripture*. Grand Rapids: Eerdmans, 1994.

Niesel, Wilhelm. *The Theology of John Calvin*. Trans. Harold Knight. Philadelphia: The Westminster Press, 1956.

Oberman, Heiko A. "*Initia Calvini*: The Matrix of Calvin's Reformation" in *Calvinus Sacrae Scripturae Professor: Calvin as Confessor of Holy Scripture*. Ed. Wilhelm H. Neuser. Grand Rapids: Eerdmans, 1994, 113–54.

Parker, T. H. L. *Calvin's Doctrine of the Knowledge of God*. Edinburgh: Oliver Boyd, 1969.

Partee, Charles. *The Theology of John Calvin*. Louisville: Westminster John Knox Press, 2008.

Robinson, Marilynne. *The Death of Adam: Essays on Modern Thought*. New York: Picador, 1998.

Torrance, T. F. *Calvin's Doctrine of Man*. Westport, Conn.: Greenwood Press, 1957, 1977.

Wallace, Ronald S. *Calvin's Doctrine of the Christian Life*. Tyler, Tex.: Geneva Divinity School Press, 1953, 1982.

————. *Calvin's Doctrine of the Word and Sacrament*. Tyler, Tex.: Geneva Divinity School Press, 1953, 1982.

Walzer, Michael. *The Revolution of the Saints: A Study in the Origin of Radical Politics*. New York: Athenum, 1974.

Weber, Max. *The Protestant Ethic and the Spirit of Capitalism*. Trans. Talcott Parsons. New York: Charles Scribner's Sons, 1958.

Zachman, Randall C. *John Calvin as Teacher, Pastor, and Theologian*. Grand Rapids: Baker Academic, 2006.

NOTES

1. Life

1. Wilhelm Baum, Edward Cunitz, and Edward Reuss, eds., *Ioannis Calvini opera quae supersunt omnia*, vols. 29–87, *Corpus Reformatorum* (Brunsvigae: Schwestschke Bruhn, 1863–1900). Hereafter CO. See also Peter Barth, Wilhelm Niesel, and Dora Scheuner, eds., *Ioannis Calvini opera selecta*, 5 vols. (Munich: Kaiser, 1526–1552).

2. Quoted in John T. McNeill, *The History and Character of Calvinism* (Oxford: Oxford University Press, 1954), 178.

3. The first biographies of Calvin are by Theodore Beza, his colleague and successor in Geneva, and Nicolas Colladon. Beza published his "Life of Calvin" in August 1564, just three months after Calvin's death, and then revised it in 1575. Colladon's "Life" was written in 1565. For the three lives, see CO 21:21–172. For an English translation of Beza's biography, see "Life of John Calvin" in John Calvin, *Tracts and Treatises on the Reformation of the Church*, 3 vols., trans. Henry Beveridge (Grand Rapids: Eerdmans, 1958), 1:lvii-cxxxviii. Hereafter, *T&T*.

4. Beza, "Life" in *T&T*, 1:cxxxviii; Alister E. McGrath, *A Life of John Calvin: A Study in the Shaping of Western Culture* (Oxford: Blackwell, 1990), 17.

5. Beza, "Life" in *T&T*, 1:cxxxv.

6. Although Calvin's brief stay at College de La Marche has become a fixture in Calvin biographies, McGrath has raised important questions about whether Calvin ever studied there. McGrath, *Calvin*, 21–27.

7. William J. Bouwsma, *John Calvin: A Sixteenth Century Portrait* (New York and Oxford: Oxford University Press, 1988), 13.

8. CO, 31:32; Francois Wendel, *Calvin: The Origins and Development of His Religious Thought*, trans. Philip Mairet (New York: Harper & Row, 1963), 37.

9. For a sampling of the discussion of the questions surrounding Calvin's "conversion," see Wendel, *Calvin*, 37–45; T. H. L. Parker, *John Calvin: A Biography* (Philadelphia: The Westminster Press, 1975), 162–66; and Alexandre Ganoczy, *The Young Calvin*, trans. David L. Foxglover and Wade Provo (Philadelphia: Westminster Press, 1987), 241–66.

10. Wendel dates Calvin's conversion at some point between a previous visit to Noyon on August 23, 1533, and the visit in May 1534. Wendel, *Calvin*, 39–40.

11. "Confession of Faith which all the citizens and inhabitants of Geneva and the subjects of the country must promise to keep and hold" in *Calvin: Theological Treatises*, ed. and trans. J. K. S. Reid, "The Library of Christian Classics" (Philadelphia: The Westminster Press, 1954), 26–33. Hereafter CTT.

12. Ibid., 31–32.

13. "Articles Concerning the Organization of the Church and of Worship at Geneva proposed by the Ministers at the Council January 16, 1537" in *CTT*, 47–55.

14. Ibid., 50–51.

15. Ibid., 52.

16. Ibid., 53.

17. Ibid., 54.

18. John Calvin, *Instruction in Faith (1537)*, trans. Paul T. Fuhrmann (Louisville: Westminster/John Knox Press, 1977, 1992), 21.

19. Ibid., 241.

20. Bernard Cottret, *Calvin: A Biography*, trans. M. Wallace McDonald (Grand Rapids: William B. Eerdmans Publishing Company, 1995), 178–81.

21. Beza, "Life" in *T&T*, 1:cxxxv.

2. The Knowledge of God

1. François Wendel, *Calvin: The Origins and Development of His Religious Thought*, trans. Philip Mairet (New York: Harper & Row, 1963), 151.

2. Ibid., 154.

3. I. John Hesselink summarizes Walter Kreck's four motifs concerning the Word of God in Calvin's theology and then adds ten topics that give Calvin's theology its distinctive character. See his essay "Calvin's Theology" in *The Cambridge Companion to John Calvin*, ed. Donald K. McKim (Cambridge: Cambridge University Press, 2004), 74–92.

4. Edward A. Dowey, Jr., for example, refers to the knowledge of God as "the foundation of Calvin's theological writing" in *The Knowledge of God in Calvin's Theology* (New York: Columbia University Press, 1952), 41.

5. John Calvin, *Institution of the Christian Religion*, trans. Ford Lewis Battles (Atlanta: John Knox Press, 1975), 20.

6. John Calvin, *Institutes of the Christian Religion*, ed. John T. McNeill, trans. Ford Lewis Battles, "The Library of Christian Classics," vols. 20 and 21 (Philadelphia: The Westminster Press, 1960), 35 (I, 1, 1).

7. Ibid.

8. Ibid., 37 (I, 1, 2).

9. Ibid., 39 (I, 1 3).

10. Ibid., 43 (I, 3, 1), 47 (I, 4, 1). Or as Calvin put it in the first article of his 1537 *Instruction in Faith*, "As no man is found, however barbarous and even savage he may be, who is not touched by some idea of religion, it is clear that we are all created in order that we may know the majesty of our creator, that having known it, we may esteem it above all and honor it with all awe, love, and reverence." John Calvin, *Instruction in Faith* (1537), ed. Paul T. Fuhrmann (Louisville: Westminster John Knox Press, 1992), 21.

11. Calvin, *Institutes*, 39 (I, 2, 1).

12. Ibid., 41–42 (I, 2, 2).

13. Ibid., 40 (I, 2, 1).

14. Ibid.

15. Two books published within months of each other debate these points and the proper interpretation of what Calvin means by the knowledge of God. See Dowey, *The Knowledge of God in Calvin's Theology* and T. H. L. Parker, *The Doctrine of the Knowledge of God: A Study in the Theology of John Calvin* (Grand Rapids: Eerdmans, 1952). Second revised edition published as *Calvin's Doctrine of the Knowledge of God* (Edinburgh: Oliver & Boyd, 1969).

16. Calvin, *Institutes*, 40 (I, 2, 1).

17. Ibid., 70–71 (I, 6, 1).

18. Ibid., 41 (I, 2, 1).

19. According to Anthony N. S. Lane, "Calvin's teaching was to a considerable extent, if not to the extent that he actually claimed a revival of Augustinianism, and it is natural therefore that he should have felt inclined to give considerable authority to Augustine." *John Calvin: Student of the Church Fathers* (Grand Rapids: Basic Books, 1999), 38.

20. Calvin, *Institutes*, 541 (III, 1, 4) and 551 (III, 2, 7).

21. Ibid., 52 (I, 5, 1).

22. Ibid., 52–53 (I, 5, 1).

23. Ibid., 54 (I, 5, 3).

24. Ibid., 55 (I, 5, 4).

25. John Calvin, *The Epistles of Paul the Apostle to the Romans and to the Thessalonians.* "Calvin's New Testament Commentaries," trans. Ross Mackenzie (Grand Rapids: William B. Eerdmans Publishing Company, 1960), 31.

26. Calvin, *Institutes*, 45 (I, 3, 2).

27. Emil Brunner, *Nature and Grace: A Contribution to the Discussion with Karl Barth* in *Natural Theology: Comprising "Nature and Grace" by Professor Dr. Emil Brunner and "No!" by Dr. Karl Barth*, trans. Peter Fraenkel, intro. John Baillie (Eugene, Ore.: Wipf and Stock Publishers, 2002), 28.

28. Ibid., 32.

29. Karl Barth, *No! Answer to Emil Brunner* in *Natural Theology*, 74–75.

30. Ibid., 104.

3. A Lamp and a Mirror

1. Calvin, *Institutes of the Christian Religion*, ed. John T. McNeill, trans. Ford Lewis Battles, "The Library of Christian Classics" (Philadelphia: The Westminster Press, 1960), 68 (I, 5, 14).

2. Ibid., 47(I, 4, 1).

3. Ibid., 65 (I, 5, 12).

4. Ibid., 70 (I, 6, 1).

5. Ibid.

6. Ibid., 83 (I, 8, 2).

7. Ibid.70 (I, 6, 1).

8. Ibid., 72 (I, 6, 2).

9. Ibid.

10. Ibid., 78 (I, 7, 4).

11. Ibid., 79 (I, 7, 4).

12. Ibid., 93 (I, 9, 1).

13. John Calvin, *Against the Fantastic and Furious Sect of the Libertines Who Are Called "Spirituals"* in *Treatises Against the Anabaptists and Against the Libertines*, ed. Benjamin Wirt Farley (Grand Rapids: Baker Book House, 1982), 222.

14. Ibid., 223–24.

15. Ibid., 224.

16. We may, Calvin writes, "embrace the Spirit with no fear of being deceived when we recognize him in his own image, namely, in the Word." Calvin, *Institutes*, 95 (I, 9, 3).

17. Ibid., 347 (II, 6, 4).

18. Ibid., 121 (I, 13, 1).

19. John Calvin, *The Epistle of Paul the Apostle to the Hebrews and First and Second Epistles of St. Peter* in *Calvin's New Testament Commentaries*, ed. David W. Torrance and Thomas F. Torrance (Grand Rapids: William B. Eerdmans Publishing Company, 1963), 250.

20. Calvin, *Institutes*, 352 (I, 7, 4).

21. Ibid., 355 (II, 7, 7).

22. Ibid., 357 (II, 7, 8).

23. Ibid., 358 (II, 7, 10).

24. Ibid., 360–61 (II, 7, 12).

25. Chapter 1 of "The Westminster Confession of Faith" in *Book of Confessions: Study Edition* of the Presbyterian Church (U.S.A.) (Louisville: Geneva Press, 1996), 173–76 (6.001-6.010).

26. Calvin, *Institutes*, 70 (I, 6, 1); 71 (I, 6, 2).

27. Ibid., 74 (I, 7, 1).

4. God's Good Will

1. John Calvin, *Institutes of the Christian Religion*, ed. John T. McNeill, trans. Ford Lewis Battles, "The Library of Christian Classics," vols. 20 and 21 (Philadelphia: The Westminster Press), 72–73 (I, 6, 2–3).

2. Ibid., 131 (I, 13, 9) and 123 (I, 13, 2).

3. Ibid., 123 (I, 13, 2).

4. Ibid., 122 (I, 13, 2).

5. Ibid., 123 (I, 13, 2–3).

6. Ibid., 128 (I, 13, 6).

7. Ibid., 151 (I, 13, 24) and 144 (I, 13, 20).

8. Ibid., 161–62 (I, 14, 2).

9. Ibid., 549 (III, 2, 6); italics mine.

10. Ibid., 575 (III, 2, 29).

11. John Calvin, *The Gospel According to John, 1–10. Calvin's New Testament Commentaries*, trans. T. H. L. Parker (Grand Rapids: William B. Eerdmans Publishing Company, 1959), 73.

12. Calvin, *Institutes*, 61 (I, 5, 8). Other examples of Calvin's use of "theater" to describe creation in the *Institutes* are 72 (I, 6, 2); 179 (I, 14, 20); and 341 (II, 6, 1).

13. Ibid., 183 (I, 15, 1).

14. Ibid., 182 (I, 14, 22).

15. Ibid., 166 (I, 14, 6).

16. Ibid., 174 (I, 14, 15) and 173 (I, 14, 13).

17. Ibid.,178 (I, 14, 19).

18. Ibid., 181 (I, 14, 21–22).

19. Ibid., 184 (I, 15, 2).

20. Ibid., 194–95 (I, 15, 7–8).

21. Ibid., 195 (I, 15, 8).

22. Ibid., 197–98 (I, 16, 1); see also 204 (I, 16, 5) and 219 (I, 17, 6). See also Calvin's comments on this text in *A Harmony of the Gospels: Matthew, Mark and Luke*. 3 vols. *Calvin's New Testament Commentaries*, trans. A. W. Morrison (Grand Rapids: William B. Eerdmans Publishing Company, 1972), 1:307.

23. Calvin, *Institutes*, 198–99 (I, 16, 2).

24. Calvin, *A Harmony of the Gospels*, 1:307.

25. Calvin, *Institutes*, 210 (I, 17, 1). See also 221–22 (I, 17, 9).

26. Ibid., 200 (I, 16, 3).

27. Ibid., 202 (I, 16, 4).

28. Ibid., 204 (I, 16, 5).

29. "Catechism of the Church of Geneva" in *Calvin: Theological Treatises*, ed. J. K. S Reid. "Library of Christian Classics" (Philadelphia: The Westminster Press, 1954), 126.

30. Calvin, *Institutes*, 234 (I, 18, 3).

31. Ibid.

32. Ibid., 217 (I, 17, 5).

33. Ibid., 219 (I, 17, 7).

34. *The Book of Confessions*, Presbyterian Church (USA). "The Heidelberg Catechism," 4.026, 32.

35. For an assessment of Calvin's doctrine of providence by a contemporary theologian and an attempt to reconstruct it by means of process theology, see Langdon Gilkey, *Reaping the Whirlwind: A Christian Interpretation of History* (New York: The Seabury Press, 1976), 175–87.

5. The Mediator as Prophet, Priest, and King

1. John Calvin, *Institutes of the Christian Religion*, ed. John T. McNeill, trans. Ford Lewis Battles, "The Library of Christian Classics," vols. 20 and 21 (Philadelphia: The Westminster Press), 189, 190 (I, 15, 4).

2. Ibid., 189 (I, 15, 4).

3. Ibid., 243 (II, 1, 2).

4. Ibid.

5. Ibid., 245 (II, 1, 4).

6. Ibid., 251 (II, 1, 8).

7. John Calvin, *The Gospel According to St. John: Part One: 1-10* in *Calvin's New Testament Commentaries*, trans. T. H. L. Parker (Grand Rapids: William B. Eerdmans Publishing Company, 1959), 67.

8. Calvin, *Institutes*, 251 (II, 1, 8).

9. Ibid., 253 (II, 1, 9).

10. Ibid., 298 (II, 3, 6).

11. Ibid., 306 (II, 2, 11).

12. Ibid., 345 (II, 6, 3); italics mine.

13. Ibid., 551 (III, 2, 7).

14. Ibid., 464 (II, 12, 1).

15. Ibid., 465 (II, 12, 1).

16. Ibid., 464 (II, 12, 1).

17. Ibid., 465 (II, 12, 2).

18. Ibid.

19. Ibid., 470 (II, 12, 5).

20. Ibid., 467 (II, 12, 4).

21. Ibid.

22. Ibid.

23. "The Geneva Catechism" in *Calvin: Theological Treatises*, 95.

24. Calvin, *Institutes*, 496 (II, 15, 2).

25. Ibid., 502 (II, 15, 6).

26. Ibid.

27. Ibid., 509 (II, 16, 5). So too Calvin uses the imagery of debt and payment to describe Christ's satisfaction. Christ was subject to God's law in order to "acquire righteousness for us, undertaking to pay what we could not pay." Ibid., 533 (II, 17, 5).

28. Ibid., 466 (II, 12, 3).

29. Ibid., 505, 504 (II, 16, 2).

30. Ibid., 506 (II, 16, 3).

31. Ibid., 482 (II, 14, 1).

32. Ibid., 484 (II, 14, 3).

33. Ibid., 481 (II, 13, 4).

34. Wilhelm Niesel, *The Theology of Calvin*, trans. Harold Knight (Grand Rapids: Baker Book House, 1956), 119.

35. Calvin, *Institutes*, 484 (II, 14, 2).

36. Moltmann's argument against God's impassibility is a frequent theme in his work. See *The Crucified God*, trans. R. A. Wilson and John Bowden (London: SCM, 1974), 267–78, and *The Trinity and the Kingdom of God*, trans. Margaret Kohl (San Francisco: Harper & Row, 1981), 21–42.

6. The Efficacious Spirit

1. John Calvin, *Institutes of the Christian Religion*, ed. John T. McNeill, trans. Ford Lewis Battles, "The Library of Christian Classics," vols. 20 and 21 (Philadelphia: The Westminster Press), 537 (III, 1, 1).

2. Ibid., 561 (III, 2, 16).

3. H. Richard Niebuhr, *The Meaning of Revelation* (New York: Macmillan, 1941), 69.

4. Benjamin B. Warfield, "John Calvin the Theologian" in *Calvin and Augustine*, ed. Samuel G. Craig (Grand Rapids: Baker Book House, 1956), 484. "It is probable however that Calvin's greatest contribution to theological science lies in the rich development which he gives—and which he was first to give—to the doctrine of the work of the Holy Spirit" (485). And "above everything else he deserves, therefore, the great name of *the theologian* of the Holy Spirit" (487).

5. Calvin, *Institutes*, 538 (III, 1, 1).

6. Ibid., 539 (III, 1, 2).

7. Ibid., 541 (III, 1, 4).

8. Ibid., 549 (III, 2, 6).

9. Ibid., 583 (III, 2, 35).

10. Ibid., 592 (III, 3, 1).

11. Ibid., 593 (III, 3, 1).

12. Dietrich Bonhoeffer, *The Cost of Discipleship*, rev. ed. (New York: Macmillan, 1959), 45–47.

13. Calvin, *Institutes*, 593 (III, 3, 1).

14. Ibid., 597 (III, 3, 5).

15. Ibid., 601 (III, 3, 9).

16. Ibid., 686 (III, 6, 3).

17. Ibid., 690 (III, 7, 1).

18. Ibid., 696 (III, 7, 6).

19. John Calvin, *A Harmony of the Gospels: Matthew, Mark, and Luke*. 3 vols, trans. T. H. L. Parker (Grand Rapids: William B. Eerdmans Publishing Company, 1972), 2:194.

20. Calvin, *Institutes*, 715 (III, 9, 3).

21. Ibid., 725 (III, 11, 1).

22. Ibid., 727 (III, 11, 2).

23. Ibid., 833 (III, 19, 1).

24. See chapter 3, "Gospel and Law," 22–23.

25. Martin Luther, "The Freedom of the Christian" in *Luther's Works*, "Career of the Reformer, I," American ed., ed. Harold J. Grim (Philadelphia: Fortress Press, 1957), 3:344.

26. Calvin, *Institutes*, 841 (III, 19, 9).

27. Ibid., 723 (III, 10, 5).

28. Ibid., 845 (III, 19, 12).

29. Ibid., 851 (III, 20, 2).

30. François Wendel, *Calvin: The Origins and Development of His Religious Thought*, trans. Philip Mairet (New York: Harper & Row, 1963), 268.

31. Calvin, *Institutes*, 920–21 (III, 21, 1).

32. Ibid., 921 (III, 21, 1).

33. Ibid., 926 (III, 21, 5).

34. Ibid., 956 (III, 23, 8).

35. Ibid., 957 (III, 23, 8).

36. Ibid., 950 (III, 23, 2).

37. Ibid., 957 (III, 23, 8).

38. Ibid.

39. Friedrich Schleiermacher, *The Christian Faith*, trans. H. R. Mackintosh and J. S. Stewart (Edinburgh: T.&T. Clark, 1928), 558 (#120.4).

40. Ibid., 539 (#118.1); italics mine.

41. Ibid., 549 (#119.3).

42. Calvin, *Institutes*, 970 (III, 24, 5).

7. Mother Church

1. John Calvin, *Institutes of the Christian Religion*, ed. John T. McNeill, trans. Ford Lewis Battles, "The Library of Christian Classics," vols. 20 and 21 (Philadelphia: The Westminster Press), 1011 (IV, 1, 1); 537 (III, 1, 1); 541 (III, 1, 3).

2. Ibid., 1012 (IV, 1, 1).

3. Ibid., 1016 (IV, 1, 4).

4. Ibid., 1013 (IV, 1, 2).

5. A formulation I learned from Daniel L. Migliore of Princeton Theological Seminary.

6. Calvin, *Institutes*, 1018 (IV, 1, 5).

7. Ibid., 1016 (IV, 1, 4).

8. Ibid., 1021 (IV, 1, 7).

9. Ibid.

10. Ibid., 1031–32 (IV, 1, 17).

11. Ibid., 1023 (IV, 1, 9).

12. Ibid., 1025 (IV, 1, 11).

13. Ibid., 1031 (IV, 1, 16).

14. Ibid., 1229–54 (IV, 12).

15. Ibid., 1240 (IV, 12, 13).

16. Ibid., 1244 (IV, 12, 18).

17. Jan Milič Lochman, *The Faith of the Church*, trans. David Lewis (Philadelphia: Fortress Press, 1984), 204–5.

18. Calvin, *Institutes*, 1277 (IV, 14, 1).

19. Ibid., 1278 (IV, 14, 3).

20. Ibid., 1281 (IV, 14, 6).

21. Ibid., 1286 (IV, 14, 10).

22. Ibid., 1280 (IV, 14, 5).

23. Ibid., 1284 (IV, 14, 9).

24. Ibid., 1307 (IV, 15, 5).

25. Ibid., 1308 (I, 15, 6).

26. Ibid., 1333 (IV, 16, 10).

27. Ibid., 1330 (IV, 16, 7).

28. Ibid., 1331 (IV, 16, 8).

29. Ibid.

30. Ibid., 1403 (IV, 17, 32).

31. B. A. Gerrish, *Grace and Gratitude: The Eucharistic Theology of John Calvin* (Minneapolis: Fortress Press, 1993), 134, 132, 159, and ix. Gerrish may well be right about the eucharistic shape of Calvin's theology. It is one thing, however, to say Calvin's theology is shaped by his understanding of the Eucharist; another possibility is that his understanding of the Eucharist is shaped by his theology.

32. Ibid., 135–39.

8. Calvin and His Children

1. Andrew Pettegree, ed. *The Reformation World* (New York: Routledge, 2000); Andrew Pettegree, Alastair Duke, and Gillian Lewis, eds., *Calvinism in Europe: A Collection of Documents, 1540–1620* (New York: Cambridge University Press, 1994); Salvatore Caponetto, *The Protestant Reformation in Sixteenth Century Italy* (Kirksville, Mo.: Thomas Jefferson University Press, 1999); Karin Maag, ed.. *The Reformation in Eastern and Central Europe* (Brookfield, Vt.: Ashgate, 1997); and Graeme Murdock, *Calvinism on the Frontier, 1600–1660: International Calvinism and the Reformed Church in Hungary and Transylvania* (New York: Oxford University Press, 2000).

2. Lukas Vischer, ed., *Reformed Witness Today: A Collection of Confessions and Statements of Faith Issued by Reformed Churches*. Berne: Evangelische Arbeitsstelle Oekumene Schweiz, 1982.

3. Max Weber, *The Protestant Ethic and the Spirit of Capitalism*, trans. Talcott Parsons (New York: Charles Scribner's Sons, 1958).

4. Michael Walzer, *The Revolution of the Saints: A Study in the Origins of Radical Politics* (New York: Atheneum, 1974), 2.

5. Ibid., 303. The relation of Puritanism to the liberal world, Walzer argues, "is perhaps one of historical preparation, but not all of theoretical contribution."

6. Ibid., 300.

7. Calvin, "Prefatory Address to King Francis I of France," *Institutes*, 9.

8. Ibid., 11.

9. Ibid., 10.

10. Ibid., 1487 (IV, 20, 2).

11. Ibid., 1487 (IV, 20, 2) and 1488 (IV, 20, 3).

12. Ibid., 1488 (IV, 20, 3).

13. Ibid.

14. Ibid., 1489 (IV, 20, 4).

15. Ibid., 1518 (IV, 20, 31).

16. Ibid., 1520 (IV, 20, 32).

17. Ibid., 1521 (IV, 20, 32).

18. Ibid., 1493 (IV, 20, 8).

19. William J. Bouwsma, *John Calvin: A Sixteenth Century Portrait* (New York: Oxford University Press, 1988), 32, 230–31.

20. "The Theological Declaration of Barmen" in the *Book of Confessions (Study Edition)* of the Presbyterian Church (U.S.A.) (Louisville: Geneva Press, 1996), 311 (8.18).

21. G. D. Cloete and D. J. Smit, eds., *A Moment of Truth: The Confession of the Dutch Reformed Mission Church 1982* (Grand Rapids: William B. Eerdmans Publishing Company, 1984), 3.

Name and Subject Index